D0933603

Don't Sweat
the Small Stuff...
and It's
All Small Stuff

Dr. Richard Carlson

NEW YORK

Don't Sweat the Small Stuff... and It's All Small Stuff

SIMPLE WAYS TO KEEP THE LITTLE

THINGS FROM TAKING OVER YOUR LIFE

Library of Congress Cataloging-In-Publication Data

Carlson, Richard, 1961–
Don't sweat the small stuff—and it's all small stuff / by
Richard Carlson.—1st ed.
p.   cm.
Includes bibliographical references (p.   ).
ISBN 0-7868-8185-2
1. Behavior modification.   2. Self-management (Psychology)
3. Peace of mind.   4. Stress management.   5. Self-defeating behavior.
6. Interpersonal relations.   I. Title.
BF637.B4C35   1997
158'.1—dc20   96-13822
                                                                        CIP

Designed by Jennifer Ann Daddio

GIFT EDITION
ISBN 0-7868-6410-9

3 5 7 9 10 8 6 4 2

I dedicate this book to my daughters, Jazzy and Kenna, who remind me every day how important it is to remember not to "sweat the small stuff." I love you both so much. Thank you for being just the way you are.

Acknowledgments

I would like to acknowledge the following people for assisting me in the creation of this book: Patti Breitman for her enthusiasm and encouragement surrounding this book and for her dedication and wisdom in not sweating the small stuff. And Leslie Wells for her vision and for her insightful editorial skill. Thank you both very much.

Contents

Don't Sweat
the Small Stuff...
and It's
All Small Stuff

Introduction

The greatest discovery of my generation is that a human being can alter his life by altering his attitude.

—WILLIAM JAMES

Whenever we're dealing with bad news, a difficult person, or a disappointment of some kind, most of us get into certain habits, ways of reacting to life—particularly adversity—that don't serve us very well. We overreact, blow things out of proportion, hold on too tightly, and focus on the negative aspects of life. When we are immobilized by little things—when we are irritated, annoyed, and easily bothered—our (over-) reactions not only make us frustrated but actually get in the way of getting what we want. We lose sight of the bigger picture, focus on the negative, and annoy other people who might otherwise help us. In short, we live our lives as if they were one great big emergency! We often rush around looking busy, trying to solve problems, but in reality, we are often compounding them. Because everything seems like such a big deal, we end up spending our lives dealing with one drama after another.

After a while, we begin to believe that everything really *is*

1

a big deal. We fail to recognize that the way we relate to our problems has a lot to do with how quickly and efficiently we solve them. As I hope you will soon discover, when you learn the habit of responding to life with more ease, problems that seemed "insurmountable" will begin to seem more manageable. And even the "biggies," things that are truly stressful, won't throw you off track as much as they once did.

Happily, there is another way to relate to life—a softer, more graceful path that makes life seem easier and the people in it more compatible. This "other way" of living involves replacing old habits of "reaction" with new habits of perspective. These new habits enable us to have richer, more satisfying lives.

I'd like to share a personal story that touched my heart and reinforced an important lesson—a story that demonstrates the essential message of this book. As you will see, the events of this story planted the seed for the title of the book you are about to read.

About a year ago a foreign publisher contacted me and requested that I attempt to get an endorsement from best-selling author Dr. Wayne Dyer for a foreign edition of my book *You Can Feel Good Again.* I told them that while Dr. Dyer had given me an endorsement for an earlier book, I had no idea whether or not he would consider doing so again. I told them, however, that I would try.

As is often the case in the publishing world, I sent out my request, but did not hear back. After some time had gone by, I came to the conclusion that Dr. Dyer was either too busy or unwilling to write an endorsement. I honored this decision and let the publisher know that we wouldn't be able to use his name to promote the book. I considered the case closed.

About six months later, however, I received a copy of the foreign edition and to my surprise, right on the cover was the old endorsement for the earlier book from Dr. Dyer! Despite my specific instructions to the contrary, the foreign publisher had used his earlier quote and transferred it to the new book. I was extremely upset, and worried about the implications as well as the possible consequences. I called my literary agent, who immediately contacted the publisher and demanded that the books be taken off the shelves.

In the meantime, I decided to write Dr. Dyer an apology, explaining the situation and all that was being done to rectify the problem. After a few weeks of wondering about what his response might be, I received a letter in the mail that said the following: "Richard. There are two rules for living in harmony. #1) Don't sweat the small stuff and #2) It's all small stuff. Let the quote stand. Love, Wayne."

That was it! No lectures, no threats. No hard feelings and no confrontation. Despite the obvious unethical use of his very famous name, he responded with grace and humility; no feathers ruffled. His response demonstrated the important concepts of "going with the flow," and of learning to respond to life gracefully, with ease.

For more than a decade I have worked with clients, helping them to approach life in this more accepting way. Together, we deal with all types of issues—stress, relationship problems, work-related issues, addictions, and general frustration.

In this book, I will share with you very specific strategies—things you can start doing today—that will help you respond to life more gracefully. The strategies you are going to read about are the ones that have proven themselves to be the most successful by clients and readers of mine over the years. They also represent the way I like to approach my own life: the path of least resistance. Each strategy is simple, yet powerful, and will act as a navigational guide to point you in the direction of greater perspective and more relaxed living. You'll find that many of the strategies will apply not only to isolated events but to many of life's most difficult challenges.

When you "don't sweat the small stuff," your life won't be perfect, but you *will* learn to accept what life has to offer with far less resistance. As we learn in the Zen philosophy, when you learn to "let go" of problems instead of resisting with all your might, your life will begin to flow. You will, as the serenity prayer suggests, "Change the things that can be changed, accept those that cannot, and have the wisdom to know the difference." I'm confident that if you give these strategies a try, you will learn the two rules of harmony. #1) Don't sweat the small stuff, and #2) It's all small stuff. As you incorporate these ideas into your life you will begin to create a more peaceful and loving you.

1.

Don't Sweat the Small Stuff

Often we allow ourselves to get all worked up about things that, upon closer examination, *aren't* really that big a deal. We focus on little problems and concerns and blow them way out of proportion. A stranger, for example, might cut in front of us in traffic. Rather than let it go, and go on with our day, we convince ourselves that we are justified in our anger. We play out an imaginary confrontation in our mind. Many of us might even tell someone else about the incident later on rather than simply let it go.

Why not instead simply allow the driver to have his accident somewhere else? Try to have compassion for the person and remember how painful it is to be in such an enormous hurry. This way, we can maintain our own sense of well-being and avoid taking other people's problems personally.

There are many similar, "small stuff" examples that occur every day in our lives. Whether we had to wait in line, listen to unfair criticism, or do the lion's share of the work, it pays enormous dividends if we learn not to worry about little things. So many people spend so much of their life energy "sweating the small stuff" that they completely lose touch with the magic and beauty of life. When you commit to working toward this goal you will find that you will have far more energy to be kinder and gentler.

2.

Make Peace with Imperfection

I've yet to meet an absolute perfectionist whose life was filled with inner peace. The need for perfection and the desire for inner tranquility conflict with each other. Whenever we are attached to having something a certain way, better than it already is, we are, almost by definition, engaged in a losing battle. Rather than being content and grateful for what we have, we are focused on what's wrong with something and our need to fix it. When we are zeroed in on what's wrong, it implies that we are dissatisfied, discontent.

Whether it's related to ourselves—a disorganized closet, a scratch on the car, an imperfect accomplishment, a few pounds we would like to lose—or someone else's "imperfections"—the way someone looks, behaves, or lives their life—the very act of focusing on imperfection pulls us away from our goal of being kind and gentle. This strategy has nothing to do with ceasing to do your very best but with being overly attached and focused on what's wrong with life. It's about realizing that while there's always a better way to do something, this doesn't mean that you can't enjoy and appreciate the way things already are.

The solution here is to catch yourself when you fall into your habit of insisting that things should be other than they are. Gently remind yourself that life is okay the way it is, right now. In the absence of your judgment, everything would be fine. As you begin to eliminate your need for perfection in all areas of your life, you'll begin to discover the perfection in life itself.

3.

Let Go of the Idea that Gentle, Relaxed People Can't Be Superachievers

O ne of the major reasons so many of us remain hurried, frightened, and competitive, and continue to live life as if it were one giant emergency, is our fear that if we were to become more peaceful and loving, we would suddenly stop achieving our goals. We would become lazy and apathetic.

You can put this fear to rest by realizing that the opposite is actually true. Fearful, frantic thinking takes an enormous amount of energy and drains the creativity and motivation from our lives. When you are fearful or frantic, you literally immobilize yourself from your greatest potential, not to mention enjoyment. Any success that you do have is despite your fear, not because of it.

I have had the good fortune to surround myself with some very relaxed, peaceful, and loving people. Some of these people are best-selling authors, loving parents, counselors, computer experts, and chief executive officers. All of them are fulfilled in what they do and are very proficient at their given skills.

I have learned the important lesson: When you have what you want (inner peace), you are *less* distracted by your wants, needs, desires, and concerns. It's thus easier to concentrate, focus, achieve your goals, and to give back to others.

4.

Be Aware of the Snowball Effect of Your Thinking

A powerful technique for becoming more peaceful is to be aware of how quickly your negative and insecure thinking can spiral out of control. Have you ever noticed how uptight you feel when you're caught up in your thinking? And, to top it off, the more absorbed you get in the details of whatever is upsetting you, the worse you feel. One thought leads to another, and yet another, until at some point, you become incredibly agitated.

For example, you might wake up in the middle of the night and remember a phone call that needs to be made the following day. Then, rather than feeling relieved that you remembered such an important call, you start thinking about everything else you have to do tomorrow. You start rehearsing a probable conversation with your boss, getting yourself even more upset. Pretty soon you think to yourself, "I can't believe how busy I am. I must make fifty phone calls a day. Whose life is this any-way?" and on and on it goes until you're feeling sorry for yourself. For many people, there's no limit to how long this type of "thought attack" can go on. In fact, I've been told by clients that many of their days and nights are spent in this type of mental rehearsal. Needless to say, it's impossible to feel peaceful with your head full of concerns and annoyances.

The solution is to notice what's happening in your head before your thoughts have a chance to build any momentum. The sooner you catch yourself in the act of building your mental snowball, the easier it is to stop. In our example here, you might notice your snowball thinking right when you start running through the list of what you have to do the next day. Then, instead of obsessing on your upcoming day, you say to yourself, "Whew, there I go again," and consciously nip it in the bud. You stop your train of thought before it has a chance to get going. You can then focus, not on how overwhelmed you are, but on how grateful you are for remembering the phone call that needed to be made. If it's the middle of the night, write it down on a piece of paper and go back to sleep. You might even consider keeping a pen and paper by the bed for such moments.

You may indeed be a very busy person, but remember that

filling your head with thoughts of how overwhelmed you are only exacerbates the problem by making you feel even more stressed than you already do. Try this simple little exercise the next time you begin to obsess on your schedule. You'll be amazed at how effective it can be.

5.

Develop Your Compassion

Nothing helps us build our perspective more than developing compassion for others. Compassion is a sympathetic feeling. It involves the willingness to put yourself in someone else's shoes, to take the focus off yourself and to imagine what it's like to be in someone else's predicament, and simultaneously, to feel love for that person. It's the recognition that other people's problems, their pain and frustrations, are every bit as real as our own—often far worse. In recognizing this fact and trying to offer some assistance, we open our own hearts and greatly enhance our sense of gratitude.

Compassion is something you can develop with practice. It involves two things: intention and action. Intention simply means you remember to open your heart to others; you expand what and who matters, from yourself to other people. Action is simply the "what you do about it." You might donate a little money or time (or both) on a regular basis to a cause near to your heart. Or perhaps you'll offer a beautiful smile and genuine "hello" to the people you meet on the street. It's not so important what you do, just that you do something. As Mother Teresa reminds us, "We cannot do great things on this earth. We can only do small things with great love."

Compassion develops your sense of gratitude by taking your attention off all the little things that most of us have learned to take too seriously. When you take time, often, to reflect on the miracle of life—the miracle that you are even able to read this book—the gift of sight, of love, and all the rest, it can help to remind you that many of the things that you think of as "big stuff" are really just "small stuff" that you are *turning into* big stuff.

6.

Remind Yourself that When You Die, Your "In Basket" Won't Be Empty

So many of us live our lives as if the secret purpose is to somehow get everything done. We stay up late, get up early, avoid having fun, and keep our loved ones waiting. Sadly, I've seen many people who put off their loved ones so long that the loved ones lose interest in maintaining the relationship. I used to do this myself. Often, we convince ourselves that our obsession with our "to do" list is only temporary—that once we get through the list, we'll be calm, relaxed, and happy. But in reality, this rarely happens. As items are checked off, new ones simply replace them.

The nature of your "in basket" is that it's *meant* to have items to be completed in it—it's not meant to be empty. There will always be phone calls that need to be made, projects to complete, and work to be done. In fact, it can be argued that a full "in basket" is essential for success. It means your time is in demand!

Regardless of who you are or what you do, however, remember that *nothing* is more important than your own sense of happiness and inner peace and that of your loved ones. If you're obsessed with getting everything done, you'll never have a sense of well-being! In reality, almost everything can wait. Very little in our work lives truly falls into the "emergency" category. If you stay focused on your work, it will all get done in due time.

I find that if I remind myself (frequently) that the purpose of life *isn't* to get it all done but to enjoy each step along the way and live a life filled with love, it's far easier for me to control my obsession with completing my list of things to do. Remember, when you die, there *will* still be unfinished business to take care of. And you know what? Someone else will do it for you! Don't waste any more precious moments of your life regretting the inevitable.

7.

Don't Interrupt Others or
Finish Their Sentences

Ι t wasn't until a few years ago that I realized how often I interrupted others and/or finished their sentences. Shortly thereafter, I also realized how destructive this habit was, not only to the respect and love I received from others but also for the tremendous amount of energy it takes to try to be in two heads at once! Think about it for a moment. When you hurry someone along, interrupt someone, or finish his or her sentence, you have to keep track not only of your own thoughts but of those of the person you are interrupting as well. This tendency (which, by the way, is extremely common in busy people), encourages both parties to speed up their speech and their thinking. This, in turn, makes both people nervous, irritable, and annoyed. It's downright exhausting. It's also the cause of many arguments, because if there's one thing almost everyone resents, it's someone who doesn't listen to what they are saying. And how can you really listen to what someone is saying when you are speaking for that person?

Once you begin noticing yourself interrupting others, you'll see that this insidious tendency is nothing more than an innocent habit that has become invisible to you. This is good news because it means that all you really have to do is to begin catching yourself when you forget. Remind yourself (before a conversation begins, if possible) to be patient and wait. Tell yourself to allow the other person to finish speaking before you take your turn. You'll notice, right away, how much the interactions with the people in your life will improve as a direct result of this simple act. The people you communicate with will feel much more relaxed around you when they feel heard and listened to. You'll also notice how much more relaxed *you'll* feel when you stop interrupting others. Your heart and pulse rates will slow down, and you'll begin to enjoy your conversations rather than rush through them. This is an easy way to become a more relaxed, loving person.

8.

Do Something Nice for Someone Else—
and Don't Tell *Anyone* About It

While many of us frequently do nice things for others, we are almost certain to mention our acts of kindness to someone else, secretly seeking their approval.

When we share our own niceness or generosity with someone else, it makes us feel like we are thoughtful people, it reminds us of how nice we are and how deserving we are of kindness.

While all acts of kindness are inherently wonderful, there is something even more magical about doing something thoughtful but mentioning it to no one, ever. You always feel good when you give to others. Rather than diluting the positive feelings by telling others about your own kindness, by keeping it to yourself you get to retain *all* the positive feelings.

It's really true that one should give for the sake of giving, not to receive something in return. This is precisely what you are doing when you don't mention your kindness to others—your rewards are the warm feelings that come from the act of giving. The next time you do something really nice for someone else, keep it to yourself and revel in the abundant joy of giving.

9.

Let Others Have the Glory

There is something magical that happens to the human spirit, a sense of calm that comes over you, when you cease needing all the attention directed toward yourself and instead allow others to have the glory.

Our need for excessive attention is that ego-centered part of us that says, "Look at me. I'm special. My story is more interesting than yours." It's that voice inside of us that may not come right out and say it, but that wants to believe that "my accomplishments are slightly more important than yours." The ego is that part of us that wants to be seen, heard, respected, considered special, often at the expense of someone else. It's the part of us that interrupts someone else's story, or impatiently waits his turn to speak so that he can bring the conversation and attention back to himself. To varying degrees, most of us engage in this habit, much to our own detriment. When you immediately dive in and bring the conversation back toward you, you can subtly minimize the joy that person has in sharing, and in doing so, create distance between yourself and others. Everyone loses.

The next time someone tells you a story or shares an accomplishment with you, notice your tendency to say something about yourself in response.

Although it's a difficult habit to break, it's not only enjoyable but actually peaceful to have the quiet confidence to be able to surrender your need for attention and instead share in the joy of someone else's glory. Rather than jumping right in and saying, "Once I did the same thing" or "Guess what I did today," bite your tongue and notice what happens. Just say, "That's wonderful," or "Please tell me more," and leave it at that. The person you are speaking to will have so much more fun and, because you are so much more "present," because you are listening so carefully, he or she won't feel in competition with you. The result will be that the person will feel more relaxed around you, making him or her more confident as well as more interesting. You too will feel more relaxed because you won't be on the edge of your seat, waiting your turn.

Obviously, there are many times when it's absolutely appropriate to exchange experience back and forth, and to share *in* the glory and attention rather than giving it all away. I'm referring here to the compulsive need to grab it from others. Ironically, when you surrender your need to hog the glory, the attention you used to need from other people is replaced by a quiet inner confidence that is derived from letting others have it.

10.

Learn to Live in the Present Moment

To a large degree, the measure of our peace of mind is determined by how much we are able to live in the present moment. Irrespective of what happened yesterday or last year, and what may or may not happen tomorrow, the present moment is where you are—always!

Without question, many of us have mastered the neurotic art of spending much of our lives worrying about a variety of things—all at once. We allow past problems and future concerns to dominate our present moments, so much so that we end up anxious, frustrated, depressed, and hopeless. On the flip side, we also postpone our gratification, our stated priorities, and our happiness, often convincing ourselves that "someday" will be better than today. Unfortunately, the same mental dynamics that tell us to look toward the future will only repeat themselves so that "someday" never actually arrives. John Lennon once said, "Life is what's happening while we're busy making other plans." When we're busy making "other plans," our children are busy growing up, the people we love are moving away and dying, our bodies are getting out of shape, and our dreams are slipping away. In short, we miss out on life.

Many people live as if life were a dress rehearsal for some later date. It isn't. In fact, no one has a guarantee that he or she will be here tomorrow. Now is the only time we have, and the only time that we have any control over. When our attention is in the present moment, we push fear from our minds. Fear is the concern over events that might happen in the future—we won't have enough money, our children will get into trouble, we will get old and die, whatever.

To combat fear, the best strategy is to learn to bring your attention back to the present. Mark Twain said, "I have been through some terrible things in my life, some of which actually happened." I don't think I can say it any better. Practice keeping your attention on the here and now. Your efforts will pay great dividends.

11.

Imagine that Everyone Is Enlightened
Except You

This strategy gives you a chance to practice something that is probably completely unacceptable to you. However, if you give it a try, you might find that it's one of the most helpful exercises in self-improvement.

As the title suggests, the idea is to imagine that everyone you know and everyone you meet is perfectly enlightened. That is, everyone except you! The people you meet are all here to teach you something. Perhaps the obnoxious driver or disrespectful teenager is here to teach you about patience, the punk rocker might be here to teach you to be less judgmental.

Your job is to try to determine what the people in your life are trying to teach you. You'll find that if you do this, you'll be far less annoyed, bothered, and frustrated by the actions and imperfections of other people. You can actually get yourself in the habit of approaching life in this manner and, if you do, you'll be glad you did. Often, once you discover what someone is trying to teach you, it's easy to let go of your frustration. For example, suppose you're in the post office and the postal clerk appears to be intentionally moving slowly. Rather than feeling frustrated, ask yourself the question, "What is he trying to teach me?" Maybe you need to learn about compassion—how hard it would be to have a job that you don't like. Or perhaps you could learn a little more about being patient. Standing in line is an excellent opportunity to break your habit of feeling impatient.

You may be surprised at how fun and easy this is. All you're really doing is changing your perception from "Why are they doing this?" to "What are they trying to teach me?" Take a look around today at all the enlightened people.

12.

Let Others Be "Right" Most of the Time

O ne of the most important questions you can ever ask yourself is, "Do I want to be 'right'—or do I want to be happy?" Many times, the two are mutually exclusive!

Being right, defending our positions, takes an enormous amount of mental energy and often alienates us from the people in our lives. Needing to be right—or needing someone else to be wrong—encourages others to become defensive, and puts pressure on us to keep defending. Yet, many of us (me too, at times) spend a great deal of time and energy attempting to prove (or point out) that we are right—and/or others are wrong. Many people, consciously or unconsciously, believe that it's somehow their job to show others how their positions, statements, and points of view are incorrect, and that in doing so, the person they are correcting is going to somehow appreciate it, or at least learn something. Wrong!

Think about it. Have you *ever* been corrected by someone and said to the person who was trying to be right, "Thank you so much for showing me that I'm wrong and you're right. Now I see it. Boy, you're great!" Or, has anyone you know ever thanked you (or even agreed with you) when you corrected them, or made yourself "right" at their expense? Of course not. The truth is, all of us hate to be corrected. We all want our positions to be respected and understood by others. Being listened to and heard is one of the greatest desires of the human heart. And those who learn to listen are the most loved and respected. Those who are in the habit of correcting others are often resented and avoided.

It's not that it's *never* appropriate to be right—sometimes you genuinely need to be or want to be. Perhaps there are certain philosophical positions that you don't want to budge on such as when you hear a racist comment. Here, it's important to speak your mind. Usually, however, it's just your ego creeping in and ruining an otherwise peaceful encounter—a habit of wanting or needing to be right.

A wonderful, heartfelt strategy for becoming more peaceful and loving is to practice allowing others the joy of being right— give them the glory. Stop correcting. As hard as it may be to change this habit, it's worth any effort and practice it takes. When someone says, "I really feel it's important to . . ." rather than jumping in and saying, "No, it's more important to . . ." or any of the hundreds of other forms of conversational editing, simply let it go and allow their statement to stand. The people in your life will become less defensive and more loving. They will appreciate you more than you could ever have dreamed possible, even if they don't exactly know why. You'll discover the joy of participating in and witnessing other people's happiness, which is far more rewarding than a battle of egos. You don't have to sacrifice your deepest philosophical truths or most heartfelt opinions, but, starting today, let others be "right," *most* of the time!

13.

Become More Patient

The quality of patience goes a long way toward your goal of creating a more peaceful and loving self. The more patient you are, the more accepting you will be of what is, rather than insisting that life be exactly as you would like it to be. Without patience, life is extremely frustrating. You are easily annoyed, bothered, and irritated. Patience adds a dimension of ease and acceptance to your life. It's essential for inner peace.

Becoming more patient involves opening your heart to the present moment, even if you don't like it. If you are stuck in a traffic jam, late for an appointment, opening to the moment would mean catching yourself building a mental snowball before your thinking got out of hand and gently reminding yourself to relax. It might also be a good time to breathe as well as an opportunity to remind yourself that, in the bigger scheme of things, being late is "small stuff."

Patience also involves seeing the innocence in others. My wife, Kris, and I have two young children ages four and seven.

On many occasions while writing this book, our four-year-old daughter has walked into my office and interrupted my work, which can be disruptive to a writer. What I have learned to do (most of the time) is to see the innocence in her behavior rather than to focus on the potential implications of her interruption ("I won't get my work done, I'll lose my train of thought, this was my only opportunity to write today," and so forth). I remind myself *why* she is coming to see me—because she loves me, not because she is conspiring to ruin my work. When I remember to see the innocence, I immediately bring forth a feeling of patience, and my attention is brought back to the moment. Any irritation that may have been building is eliminated and I'm reminded, once again, of how fortunate I am to have such beautiful children. I have found that, if you look deeply enough, you can almost always see the innocence in other people as well as in potentially frustrating situations. When you do, you will become a more patient and peaceful person and, in some strange way, you begin to enjoy many of the moments that used to frustrate you.

14.

Create "Patience Practice Periods"

Patience is a quality of heart that can be greatly enhanced with deliberate practice. An effective way that I have found to deepen my own patience is to create actual practice periods—periods of time that I set up in my mind to practice the art of patience. Life itself becomes a classroom, and the curriculum is patience.

You can start with as little as five minutes and build up your capacity for patience, over time. Start by saying to yourself, "Okay, for the next five minutes I won't allow myself to be bothered by anything. I'll be patient." What you'll discover is truly amazing. Your intention to be patient, especially if you know it's only for a short while, immediately strengthens your capacity for patience. Patience is one of those special qualities where success feeds on itself. Once you reach little milestones—five minutes of successful patience—you'll begin to see that you do, indeed, have the capacity to be patient, even for longer periods of time. Over time, you may even become a patient person.

Since I have young children at home, I have many possibilities to practice the art of patience. For example, on a day when both girls are firing questions at me as I'm trying to make important phone calls, I'll say to myself, "Now is a great time to be patient. For the next half hour I'm going to be as patient as possible (see, I've worked hard, I'm up to thirty minutes)!" All kidding aside, it really works—and it has worked in our family. As I keep my cool and don't allow myself to be annoyed and upset, I can calmly, yet firmly, direct my children's behavior far more effectively than when I get crazy. The simple act of gearing my mind toward patience allows me to remain in the present moment far more than I would if I were upset, thinking about all the times this has happened before and feeling like a martyr. What's more, my patient feelings are often contagious—they rub off on the kids, who then decide, on their own, that it's no fun to bother Dad.

Being patient allows me to keep my perspective. I can remember, even in the midst of a difficult situation, that what's before me—my present challenge—isn't "life or death" but simply a minor obstacle that must be dealt with. Without patience, the same scenario can become a major emergency complete with yelling, frustration, hurt feelings, and high blood pressure. It's really not worth all that. Whether you're needing to deal with children, your boss, or a difficult person or situation—if you don't want to "sweat the small stuff," improving your patience level is a great way to start.

15.

Be the First One to Act Loving or Reach Out

So many of us hold on to little resentments that may have stemmed from an argument, a misunderstanding, the way we were raised, or some other painful event. Stubbornly, we wait for someone else to reach out to us—believing this is the *only* way we can forgive or rekindle a friendship or family relationship.

An acquaintance of mine, whose health isn't very good, recently told me that she hasn't spoken to her son in almost three years. "Why not?" I asked. She said that she and her son had had a disagreement about his wife and that she wouldn't speak to him again unless he called first. When I suggested that she be the one to reach out, she resisted initially and said, "I can't do that. He's the one who should apologize." She was literally willing to die before reaching out to her only son. After a little gentle encouragement, however, she did decide to be the first one to reach out. To her amazement, her son was grateful for her willingness to call and offered an apology of his own. As is usually the case when someone takes the chance and reaches out, everyone wins.

Whenever we hold on to our anger, we turn "small stuff" into really "big stuff" in our minds. We start to believe that our positions are more important than our happiness. They are not. If you want to be a more peaceful person you must understand that being right is almost never more important than allowing yourself to be happy. The way to be happy is to let go, and reach out. Let other people be right. This doesn't mean that you're wrong. Everything will be fine. You'll experience the peace of letting go, as well as the joy of letting others be right. You'll also notice that, as you reach out and let others be "right," they will become less defensive and more loving toward you. They might even reach back. But, if for some reason they don't, that's okay too. You'll have the inner satisfaction of knowing that you have done your part to create a more loving world, and certainly you'll be more peaceful yourself.

16.

Ask Yourself the Question,
"Will This Matter a Year from Now?"

Almost every day I play a game with myself that I call "time warp." I made it up in response to my consistent, erroneous belief that what I was all worked up about was really important.

To play "time warp," all you have to do is imagine that whatever circumstance you are dealing with isn't happening right now but a year from now. Then simply ask yourself, "Is this situation really as important as I'm making it out to be?" Once in a great while it may be—but a vast majority of the time, it simply isn't.

Whether it be an argument with your spouse, child, or boss, a mistake, a lost opportunity, a lost wallet, a work-related rejection, or a sprained ankle, chances are, a year from now you aren't going to care. It will be one more irrelevant detail in your life. While this simple game won't solve all your problems, it can give you an enormous amount of needed perspective. I find myself laughing at things that I used to take far too seriously. Now, rather than using up my energy feeling angry and overwhelmed, I can use it instead on spending time with my wife and children or engaging in creative thinking.

17.

Surrender to the Fact that Life Isn't Fair

A friend of mine, in response to a conversation we were having about the injustices of life, asked me the question, "Who said life was going to be fair, or that it was even meant to be fair?" Her question was a good one. It reminded me of something I was taught as a youngster: Life isn't fair. It's a bummer, but it's absolutely true. Ironically, recognizing this sobering fact can be a very liberating insight.

One of the mistakes many of us make is that we feel sorry for ourselves, or for others, thinking that life *should be* fair, or that someday it will be. It's not and it won't. When we make this mistake we tend to spend a lot of time wallowing and/or complaining about what's wrong with life. We commiserate with others, discussing the injustices of life. "It's not fair," we complain, not realizing that, perhaps, it was never intended to be.

One of the *nice* things about surrendering to the fact that life isn't fair is that it keeps us from feeling sorry for ourselves by encouraging us to do the very best we can with what we have. We know it's not "life's job" to make everything perfect, it's our own challenge. Surrendering to this fact also keeps us from feeling sorry for others because we are reminded that everyone is dealt a different hand, and everyone has unique strengths and challenges. This insight has helped me to deal with the problems of raising two children, the difficult decisions I've had to make about who to help and who I can't help, as well as with my own personal struggles during those times that I have felt victimized or unfairly treated. It almost always wakes me up to reality and puts me back on track.

The fact that life isn't fair doesn't mean we shouldn't do everything in our power to improve our own lives or the world as a whole. To the contrary, it suggests that we should. When we don't recognize or admit that life isn't fair, we tend to feel pity for others and for ourselves. Pity, of course, is a self-defeating emotion that does nothing for anyone, except to make everyone feel worse than they already do. When we *do* recognize that life isn't fair, however, we feel *compassion* for others and for ourselves. And compassion is a heartfelt emotion that delivers loving-kindness to everyone it touches. The next time you find yourself thinking about the injustices of the world, try reminding yourself of this very basic fact. You may be surprised that it can nudge you out of self-pity and into helpful action.

18.

Allow Yourself to Be Bored

For many of us, our lives are so filled with stimuli, not to mention responsibilities, that it's almost impossible for us to sit still and do nothing, much less relax—even for a few minutes. A friend of mine said to me, "People are no longer human beings. We should be called human doings."

I was first exposed to the idea that occasional boredom can actually be good for me while studying with a therapist in La Conner, Washington, a tiny little town with very little "to do." After finishing our first day together, I asked my instructor, "What is there to do around here at night?" He responded by saying, "What I'd like you to do is allow yourself to be bored. Do nothing. This is part of your training." At first I thought he was kidding! "Why on earth would I choose to be bored?" I asked. He went on to explain that if you allow yourself to be bored, even for an hour—or less—and don't fight it, the feelings of boredom will be replaced with feelings of peace. And after a little practice, you'll learn to relax.

Much to my surprise, he was absolutely right. At first, I could barely stand it. I was so used to doing something every second that I really struggled to relax. But after a while I got used to it, and have long since learned to enjoy it. I'm not talking about hours of idle time or laziness, but simply learning the art of relaxing, of just "being," rather than "doing," for a few minutes each day. There isn't a specific technique other than to consciously do nothing. Just sit still, perhaps look out the window and notice your thoughts and feelings. At first you may get a little anxious, but each day it will get a little easier. The payback is tremendous.

Much of our anxiety and inner struggle stems from our busy, overactive minds always needing something to entertain them, something to focus on, and always wondering "What's next?" While we're eating dinner we wonder what's for dessert. While eating dessert, we ponder what we should do afterward. After that evening, it's "What should we do this weekend?" After we've been out, we walk into the house and immediately turn on the television, pick up the phone, open a book, or start cleaning. It's almost as though we're frightened at the thought of not having something to do, even for a minute.

The beauty of doing nothing is that it teaches you to clear your mind and relax. It allows your mind the freedom to "not know," for a brief period of time. Just like your body, your mind needs an occasional break from its hectic routine. When you allow your mind to take a break, it comes back stronger, sharper, more focused and creative.

When you allow yourself to be bored, it takes an enormous amount of pressure off you to be performing and doing something every second of every day. Now, when either of my two children says to me, "Daddy, I'm bored," I respond by saying, "Great, be bored for a while. It's good for you." Once I say this, they always give up on the idea of me solving their problem. You probably never thought someone would actually suggest that you allow yourself to be bored. I guess there's a first for everything!

19.

Lower Your Tolerance to Stress

I t seems that we have it backward in our society. We tend to look up to people who are under a great deal of stress, who can handle loads of stress, and those who are under a great deal of pressure. When someone says, "I've been working really hard," or "I'm really stressed out," we are taught to admire, even emulate their behavior. In my work as a stress consultant I hear the proud words "I have a very high tolerance to stress" almost every day. It probably won't come as a surprise that when these stressed-out people first arrive at my office, more often than not, what they are hoping for are strategies to *raise* their tolerance to stress even higher so they can handle even more!

Fortunately, there is an inviolable law in our emotional environment that goes something like this: Our current level of stress will be exactly that of our tolerance to stress. You'll notice that the people who say, "I can handle lots of stress" will *always* be under a great deal of it! So, if you teach people to raise their tolerance to stress, that's exactly what will happen. They will accept even more confusion and responsibility until again, their external level of stress matches that of their tolerance. Usually it takes a crisis of some kind to wake up a stressed-out person to their own craziness—a spouse leaves, a health issue emerges, a serious addiction takes over their life—something happens that jolts them into a search for a new kind of strategy.

It may seem strange, but if you were to enroll in the average stress management workshop, what you would probably learn is to *raise* your tolerance to stress. It seems that even stress consultants are stressed out!

What you want to start doing is noticing your stress early, *before* it gets out of hand. When you feel your mind moving too quickly, it's time to back off and regain your bearings. When your schedule is getting out of hand, it's a signal that it's time to slow down and reevaluate what's important rather than power through everything on the list. When you're feeling out of control and resentful of all you have to do, rather than roll up your sleeves and "get to it," a better strategy is to relax, take a few deep breaths, and go for a short walk. You'll find that when you catch yourself getting too stressed out—early, before it gets out of control—your stress will be like the proverbial snowball rolling down the hill. When it's small, it's manageable and easy to control. Once it gathers momentum, however, it's difficult, if not impossible, to stop.

There's no need to worry that you won't get it all done. When your mind is clear and peaceful and your stress level is reduced, you'll be more effective and you'll have more fun. As you lower your tolerance to stress, you will find that you'll have far less stress to handle, as well as creative ideas for handling the stress that is left over.

20.

Once a Week, Write a Heartfelt Letter

This is an exercise that has helped to change many lives, assisting people in becoming more peaceful and loving. Taking a few minutes each week to write a heartfelt letter does many things for you. Picking up a pen or typing on a keyboard slows you down long enough to remember the beautiful people in your life. The act of sitting down to write helps to fill your life with gratitude.

Once you decide to try this, you'll probably be amazed at how many people appear on your list. I had one client who said, "I probably don't have enough weeks left in my life to write everyone on my list." This may or may not be true for you, but chances are, there are a number of people in your life, or from your past, who are quite deserving of a friendly, heartfelt letter. Even if you don't have people in your life to whom you feel you can write, go ahead and write the letter to someone you don't know instead—perhaps to an author who may not even be living, whose works you admire. Or to a great inventor or thinker from the past or present. Part of the value of the letter is to gear your thinking toward gratitude. Writing the letter, even if it isn't sent, would do just that.

The purpose of your letter is very simple: to express love and gratitude. Don't worry if you're awkward at writing letters. This isn't a contest from the head but a gift from the heart. If you can't think of much to say, start with short little notes like, "Dear Jasmine. I woke up this morning thinking of how lucky I am to have people like you in my life. Thank you so much for being my friend. I am truly blessed, and I wish for you all the happiness and joy that life can bring. Love, Richard."

Not only does writing and sending a note like this focus your attention on what's right in your life, but the person receiving it will, in all likelihood, be extremely touched and grateful. Often, this simple action starts a spiral of loving actions whereby the person receiving your letter may decide to do the same thing to someone else, or perhaps will act and feel more loving toward others. Write your first letter this week. I'll bet you'll be glad you did.

21.

Imagine Yourself
at Your Own Funeral

This strategy is a little scary for some people but universally effective at reminding us of what's most important in our lives.

When we look back on our lives, how many of us are going to be pleased at how uptight we were? Almost universally, when people look back on their lives while on their deathbed, they wish that their priorities had been quite different. With few exceptions, people wish they hadn't "sweated the small stuff" so much. Instead, they wish they had spent more time with the people and activities that they truly loved and less time worrying about aspects of life that, upon deeper examination, really don't matter all that much. Imagining yourself at your own funeral allows you to look back at your life while you still have the chance to make some important changes.

While it can be a little scary or painful, it's a good idea to consider your own death and, in the process, your life. Doing so will remind you of the kind of person you want to be and the priorities that are most important to you. If you're at all like me, you'll probably get a wake-up call that can be an excellent source of change.

22.

Repeat to Yourself,
"Life Isn't an Emergency"

In some ways, this strategy epitomizes the essential message of this book. Although most people believe otherwise, the truth is, life *isn't* an emergency.

I've had hundreds of clients over the years who have all but neglected their families as well as their own dreams because of their propensity to believe that life is an emergency. They justify their neurotic behavior by believing that if they don't work eighty hours a week, they won't get everything done. Sometimes I remind them that when they die, their "in basket" won't be empty!

A client who is a homemaker and mother of three children recently said to me, "I just can't get the house cleaned up the way I like it before everyone leaves in the morning." She was so upset over her inability to be perfect that her doctor had prescribed her anti-anxiety medicine. She was acting (and feeling) like there was a gun pointed at her head and the sniper was demanding that every dish be put away and every towel folded—or else! Again, the silent assumption was, *this is an emergency!* The truth was, no one other than she had created the pressure she was experiencing.

I've never met anyone (myself included) who hasn't turned little things into great big emergencies. We take our own goals so seriously that we forget to have fun along the way, and we forget to cut ourselves some slack. We take simple preferences and turn them into conditions for our own happiness. Or, we beat ourselves up if we can't meet our self-created deadlines. The first step in becoming a more peaceful person is to have the humility to admit that, in most cases, you're creating your own emergencies. Life will usually go on if things don't go according to plan. It's helpful to keep reminding yourself and repeating the sentence, "Life isn't an emergency."

23.

Experiment with Your Back Burner

Your back burner is an excellent tool for remembering a fact or bringing forth an insight. It's an almost effortless yet effective way of using your mind when you might otherwise start feeling stressed out. Using your back burner means allowing your mind to solve a problem while you are busy doing something else, here in the present moment.

The back burner of your mind works in the same way as the back burner of a stove. While on low heat, the cooking process mixes, blends, and simmers the ingredients into a tasty meal. The way you prepared this meal was to throw the various ingredients into the pot, mix them up, and leave them alone. Often the less you interfere, the better the result.

In much the same way, we can solve many of life's problems (serious and otherwise) if we feed the back burner of our mind with a list of problems, facts, and variables, and possible solutions. Just as when we make soup or a sauce, the thoughts and ideas we feed the back burner of our mind must be left alone to simmer properly.

Whether you are struggling to solve a problem or can't remember a person's name, your back burner is always available to help you. It puts our quieter, softer, and sometimes most intelligent source of thinking to work for us on issues that we have no immediate answer for. The back burner is *not* a prescription for denial or procrastination. In other words, while you *do* want to put your problems on your back burner, you *don't* want to turn the burner off. Instead, you want to gently hold the problem in your mind without actively analyzing it. This simple technique will help you solve many problems and will greatly reduce the stress and effort in your life.

24.

Spend a Moment Every Day Thinking of Someone to Thank

This simple strategy, which may take only a few seconds to complete, has long been one of the most important habits I have ever engaged in. I try to remember to start my day thinking of someone to thank. To me, gratitude and inner peace go hand in hand. The more genuinely grateful I feel for the gift of my life, the more peaceful I feel. Gratitude, then, is worthy of a little practice.

If you're anything like me, you probably have many people in your life to feel grateful for: friends, family members, people from your past, teachers, gurus, people from work, someone who gave you a break, as well as countless others. You may want to thank a higher power for the gift of life itself, or for the beauty of nature.

As you think of people to be grateful for, remember that it can be anyone—someone who allowed you to merge into traffic, someone who held the door open for you, or a physician who saved your life. The point is to gear your attention toward gratitude, preferably first thing in the morning.

I learned a long time ago that it's easy to allow my mind to slip into various forms of negativity. When I do, the first thing that leaves me is my sense of gratitude. I begin to take the people in my life for granted, and the love that I often feel is replaced with resentment and frustration. What this exercise reminds me to do is to focus on the good in my life. Invariably as I think of one person to feel gratitude for, the image of another person pops into my head, then another and another. Pretty soon I'm thinking of other things to be grateful for—my health, my children, my home, my career, the readers of my books, my freedom, and on and on it goes.

It may seem like an awfully simple suggestion, but it really works! If you wake up in the morning with gratitude on your mind, it's pretty difficult, in fact almost impossible, to feel anything but peace.

25.

Smile at Strangers, Look into Their Eyes, and Say Hello

Have you ever noticed or thought about how little eye contact most of us have with strangers? Why? Are we afraid of them? What keeps us from opening our hearts to people we don't know?

I don't really know the answers to these questions, but I do know that there is virtually always a parallel between our attitude toward strangers and our overall level of happiness. In other words, it's unusual to find a person who walks around with her head down, frowning and looking away from people, who is secretly a peaceful, joyful person.

I'm not suggesting it's better to be outgoing than introverted, that you need to expend tons of extra energy trying to brighten others' days, or that you should pretend to be friendly. I am suggesting, however, that if you think of strangers as being a little more like you and treat them not only with kindness and respect but with smiles and eye contact as well, you'll probably notice some pretty nice changes in yourself. You'll begin to see that most people are just like you—most of them have families, people they love, troubles, concerns, likes, dislikes, fears, and so forth. You'll also notice how nice and grateful people can be when you're the first one to reach out. When you see how similar we all are, you begin to see the innocence in all of us. In other words, even though we often mess up, most of us are doing the best that we know how with the circumstances that surround us. Along with seeing the innocence in people comes a profound feeling of inner happiness.

26.

Set Aside Quiet Time, Every Day

As I begin to write this strategy it's exactly 4:30 in the morning, my favorite time of the day. I still have at least an hour and a half before my wife and children get out of bed and the phone begins to ring; at least an hour before anyone can ask me to do anything. It's absolutely silent outside and I'm in complete solitude. There is something rejuvenating and peaceful about being alone and having some time to reflect, work, or simply enjoy the quiet.

I've been working in the stress management field for well over a decade. In that time I've met some extraordinary people. I can't think of a single person whom I would consider to be inwardly peaceful who doesn't carve out at least a little quiet time, virtually every day. Whether it's ten minutes of meditation or yoga, spending a little time in nature, or locking the bathroom door and taking a ten-minute bath, quiet time to yourself is a vital part of life. Like spending time alone, it helps to balance the noise and confusion that infiltrate much of our day.

Personally, when I set aside quiet time for myself, it makes the rest of my day seem manageable. When I don't, I really notice the difference.

There's a little ritual that I do that I've shared with many friends. Like many people, I drive to and from my office on a daily basis. On my way home from work, as I get close to my driveway, I pull my car over and stop. There is a nice spot where I can spend a minute or two looking at the view or closing my eyes and breathing. It slows me down and helps me feel centered and grateful. I've shared this strategy with dozens of people who used to complain about having "no time for quiet." They would speed into their driveways with the radio blaring in their ears. Now, with a simple shift in their actions, they enter their homes feeling much more relaxed.

27.

Imagine the People in Your Life
as Tiny Infants and
as One-Hundred-Year-Old Adults

I learned this technique almost twenty years ago. It has proven to be extremely successful for releasing feelings of irritation toward other people.

Think of someone who truly irritates you, who makes you feel angry. Now, close your eyes and try to imagine this person as a tiny infant. See their tiny little features and their innocent little eyes. Know that babies can't help but make mistakes and each of us was, at one time, a little infant. Now, roll forward the clock one hundred years. See the same person as a very old person who is about to die. Look at their worn-out eyes and their soft smile, which suggests a bit of wisdom and the admission of mistakes made. Know that each of us will be one hundred years old, alive or dead, before too many decades go by.

You can play with this technique and alter it in many ways. It almost always provides the user with some needed perspective and compassion. If our goal is to become more peaceful and loving, we certainly don't want to harbor negativity toward others.

28.

Seek First to Understand

This is adopted from one of Stephen Covey's "Seven Habits of Highly Effective People." Using this strategy is a shortcut to becoming a more content person (and you'll probably become more effective too).

Essentially, "seek first to understand" implies that you become more interested in understanding others and less in having other people understand you. It means mastering the idea that if you want quality, fulfilling communication that is nourishing to you and others, understanding others must come first. When you understand where people are coming from, what they are trying to say, what's important to them, and so forth, *being* understood flows naturally; it falls into place with virtually no effort. When you reverse this process, however (which is what most of us do most of the time), you are putting the cart before the horse. When you try to *be* understood *before* you understand, the effort you exert will be felt by you and the person or people you are trying to reach. Communication will break down, and you may end up with a battle of two egos.

I was working with a couple who had spent the first ten years of their marriage frustrated, arguing about their finances. He couldn't understand why she wanted to save every penny they earned, and she couldn't understand why he was a spendthrift. Any rationale on either position had been lost in their joint frustration. While many problems are more complex than this couple's, their solutions were relatively simple. Neither person felt understood. They needed to learn to stop interrupting each other and to listen carefully. Rather than defending their own positions, each needed to seek first to understand. This is precisely what I got them to do. He learned that she was saving to avoid her parents' financial disasters. Essentially, she was frightened of being broke. She learned that he felt embarrassed that he wasn't able to "take care of her" as well as his father did his mother. Essentially, he wanted her to be proud of him. As each learned to understand the other, their frustration with each other was replaced by compassion. Today, they have a nice balance between spending and saving.

Seeking first to understand isn't about who's right or wrong; it is a philosophy of effective communication. When you practice this method you'll notice that the people you communicate with will feel listened to, heard, and understood. This will translate into better, more loving relationships.

29.

Become a Better Listener

I grew up believing I was a good listener. And although I have become a better listener than I was ten years ago, I have to admit I'm still only an *adequate* listener.

Effective listening is more than simply avoiding the bad habit of interrupting others while they are speaking or finishing their sentences. It's being content to listen to the *entire* thought of someone rather than waiting impatiently for your chance to respond.

In some ways, the way we fail to listen is symbolic of the way we live. We often treat communication as if it were a race. It's almost like our goal is to have no time gaps between the conclusion of the sentence of the person we are speaking with and the beginning of our own. My wife and I were recently at a café having lunch, eavesdropping on the conversations around us. It seemed that no one was really listening to one another; instead they were taking turns not listening to one another. I asked my wife if I still did the same thing. With a smile on her face she said, "Only sometimes."

Slowing down your responses and becoming a better listener aids you in becoming a more peaceful person. It takes pressure from you. If you think about it, you'll notice that it takes an enormous amount of energy and is very stressful to be sitting at the edge of your seat trying to guess what the person in front of you (or on the telephone) is going to say so that you can fire back your response. But as you wait for the people you are communicating with to finish, as you simply listen more intently to what is being said, you'll notice that the pressure you feel is off. You'll immediately feel more relaxed, and so will the people you are talking to. They will feel safe in slowing down their own responses because they won't feel in competition with you for "airtime"! Not only will becoming a better listener make you a more patient person, it will also enhance the quality of your relationships. Everyone loves to talk to someone who truly listens to what they are saying.

30.

Choose Your Battles Wisely

"Choose your battles wisely" is a popular phrase in parenting but is equally important in living a contented life. It suggests that life is filled with opportunities to choose between making a big deal out of something or simply letting it go, realizing it doesn't really matter. If you choose your battles wisely, you'll be far more effective in winning those that are truly important.

Certainly there will be times when you will want or need to argue, confront, or even fight for something you believe in. Many people, however, argue, confront, and fight over practically anything, turning their lives into a series of battles over relatively "small stuff." There is so much frustration in living this type of life that you lose track of what is truly relevant.

The tiniest disagreement or glitch in your plans can be made into a big deal if your goal (conscious or unconscious) is to have everything work out in your favor. In my book, this is nothing more than a prescription for unhappiness and frustration.

The truth is, life is rarely exactly the way we want it to be, and other people often don't act as we would like them to. Moment to moment, there are aspects of life that we like and others that we don't. There are always going to be people who disagree with you, people who do things differently, and things that don't work out. If you fight against this principle of life, you'll spend most of your life fighting battles.

A more peaceful way to live is to decide consciously which battles are worth fighting and which are better left alone. If your primary goal isn't to have everything work out perfectly but instead to live a relatively stress-free life, you'll find that most battles pull you *away from* your most tranquil feelings. Is it really important that you prove to your spouse that you are right and she is wrong, or that you confront someone simply because it appears as though he or she has made a minor mistake? Does your preference of which restaurant or movie to go to matter enough to argue over it? Does a small scratch on your car really warrant a suit in small claims court? Does the fact that your neighbor won't park his car on a different part of the street have to be discussed at your family dinner table? These and thousands of other small things are what many people spend their lives fighting about. Take a look at your own list.

If it's like mine used to be, you might want to reevaluate your priorities.

If you don't want to "sweat the small stuff," it's critical that you choose your battles wisely. If you do, there will come a day when you'll rarely feel the need to do battle at all.

31.

Become Aware of Your Moods and Don't Allow Yourself to Be Fooled by the Low Ones

Your own moods can be extremely deceptive. They can, and probably do, trick you into believing your life is far worse than it really is. When you're in a good mood, life looks great. You have perspective, common sense, and wisdom. In good moods, things don't feel so hard, problems seem less formidable and easier to solve. When you're in a good mood, relationships seem to flow and communication is easy. If you are criticized, you take it in stride.

On the contrary, when you're in a bad mood, life looks unbearably serious and difficult. You have very little perspective. You take things personally and often misinterpret those around you, as you impute malignant motives into their actions.

Here's the catch: People don't realize their moods are always on the run. They think instead that their lives have suddenly become worse in the past day, or even the last hour. So, someone who is in a good mood in the morning might love his wife, his job, and his car. He is probably optimistic about his future and feels grateful about his past. But by late afternoon, if his mood is bad, he claims he hates his job, thinks of his wife as a nuisance, thinks his car is a junker, and believes he's going nowhere in his career. If you ask him about his childhood while he's in a low mood, he'll probably tell you it was extremely difficult. He will probably blame his parents for his current plight.

Such quick and drastic contrasts may seem absurd, even funny—but we're all like that. In low moods we lose our perspective and everything seems urgent. We completely forget that when we are in a good mood, everything seems so much better. We experience the *identical* circumstances—who we are married to, where we work, the car we drive, our potential, our childhood—entirely differently, depending on our mood! When we are low, rather than blaming our mood as would be appropriate, we instead tend to feel that our whole life is wrong. It's almost as if we actually believe that our lives have fallen apart in the past hour or two.

The truth is, life is almost *never* as bad as it seems when you're in a low mood. Rather than staying stuck in a bad temper, convinced you are seeing life realistically, you can learn to question your judgment. Remind yourself, "Of course I'm feeling defensive [or angry, frustrated, stressed, depressed]; I'm in a bad mood. I always feel negative when I'm low." When you're in an ill mood, learn to pass it off as simply that: an unavoidable human condition that *will* pass with time, if you leave it alone. A low mood is not the time to analyze your life. To do so is emotional suicide. If you have a legitimate problem, it will still be there when your state of mind improves. The trick is to be grateful for our good moods and graceful in our low moods—not taking them too seriously. The next time you feel low, for whatever reason, remind yourself, "This too shall pass." It will.

32.

Life Is a Test. It Is Only a Test

O ne of my favorite posters says, "Life is a test. It is only a test. Had this been a real life you would have been instructed where to go and what to do." Whenever I think of this humorous bit of wisdom, it reminds me to not take my life so seriously.

When you look at life and its many challenges as a test, or series of tests, you begin to see each issue you face as an opportunity to grow, a chance to roll with the punches. Whether you're being bombarded with problems, responsibilities, even insurmountable hurdles, when looked at as a test, you always have a chance to succeed, in the sense of rising above that which is challenging you. If, on the other hand, you see each new issue you face as a serious battle that must be won in order to survive, you're probably in for a very rocky journey. The only time you're likely to be happy is when everything is working out just right. And we all know how often that happens.

As an experiment, see if you can apply this idea to something you are forced to deal with. Perhaps you have a difficult teenager or a demanding boss. See if you can redefine the issue you face from being a "problem" to being a test. Rather than struggling with your issue, see if there is something you can learn from it. Ask yourself, "Why is this issue in my life? What would it mean and what would be involved to rise above it? Could I possibly look at this issue any differently? Can I see it as a test of some kind?"

If you give this strategy a try you may be surprised at your changed responses. For example, I used to struggle a great deal over the issue of my perception of not having enough time. I would rush around trying to get everything done. I blamed my schedule, my family, my circumstances, and anything else I could think of for my plight. Then it dawned on me. If I wanted to be happy, my goal didn't necessarily have to be to organize my life perfectly so that I had more time, but rather to see whether I could get to the point where I felt it was okay that I couldn't get everything done that I felt I must. In other words, my real challenge was to see my struggle as a test. Seeing this issue as a test ultimately helped me to cope with one of my biggest personal frustrations. I still struggle now and then about my perceived lack of time, but less than I used to. It has become far more acceptable to me to accept things as they are.

33.

Praise and Blame Are All the Same

One of the most unavoidable life lessons is having to deal with the disapproval of others. Praise and blame are all the same is a fancy way of reminding yourself of the old cliché that you'll never be able to please all the people all the time. Even in a landslide election victory in which a candidate secures 55 percent of the vote, he or she is left with 45 percent of the population that wishes someone else were the winner. Pretty humbling, isn't it?

Our approval rating from family, friends, and the people we work with isn't likely to be much higher. The truth is, everyone has their own set of ideas with which to evaluate life, and our ideas don't always match those of other people. For some reason, however, most of us struggle against this inevitable fact. We get angry, hurt, or otherwise frustrated when people reject our ideas, tell us no, or give us some other form of disapproval.

The sooner we accept the inevitable dilemma of not being able to win the approval of everyone we meet, the easier our lives will become. When you expect to be dished out your share of disapproval instead of struggling against this fact, you'll develop a helpful perspective to assist your life journey. Rather than feeling rejected by disapproval, you can remind yourself, "Here it is again. That's okay." You can learn to be pleasantly surprised, even grateful when you receive the approval you're hoping for.

I find that there are many days when I experience both praise and blame. Someone will hire me to speak and someone else won't want to; one phone call delivers good news, another announces a new issue to deal with. One of my children is happy with my behavior, the other struggles against it. Someone says what a nice guy I am, someone else thinks I'm selfish because I don't return his phone call. This back and forth, good and bad, approval and disapproval is a part of everyone's life. I'm the first to admit that I always prefer approval over disapproval. It feels better and it's certainly easier to deal with. The more content I've become, however, the less I depend on it for my sense of well-being.

34.

Practice Random Acts of Kindness

There is a bumper sticker that has been out for some time now. You see it on cars all across the nation (in fact, I have one on my own car). It says, "Practice Random Acts of Kindness and Senseless Acts of Beauty." I have no idea who thought of this idea, but I've never seen a more important message on a car in front of me. Practicing random kindness is an effective way to get in touch with the joy of giving without expecting anything in return. It's best practiced without letting anyone know what you are doing.

There are five toll bridges in the San Francisco Bay Area. A while back, some people began paying the tolls of the cars immediately behind them. The drivers would drive to the toll window, and pull out their dollar bill, only to be informed, "Your toll has been paid by the car ahead of you." This is an example of a spontaneous, random gift, something given without expectation of or demand for anything in return. You can imagine the impact that tiny gift had on the driver of the car! Perhaps it encouraged him to be a nicer person that day. Often a single act of kindness sets a series of kind acts in motion.

There is no prescription for how to practice random kindness. It comes from the heart. Your gift might be to pick up litter in your neighborhood, make an anonymous contribution to a charity, send some cash in an unmarked envelope to make someone experiencing financial stress breathe a little easier, save an animal by bringing it to an animal rescue agency, or get a volunteer position feeding hungry people at a church or shelter. You may want to do all these things, and more. The point is, giving is fun and it doesn't have to be expensive.

Perhaps the greatest reason to practice random kindness is that it brings great contentment into your life. Each act of kindness rewards you with positive feelings and reminds you of the important aspects of life—service, kindness, and love. If we all do our own part, pretty soon we will live in a nicer world.

35.

Look Beyond Behavior

Have you ever heard yourself, or someone else, say: "Don't mind John, he didn't know what he was doing"? If so, you have been exposed to the wisdom of "looking beyond behavior." If you have children, you know very well the importance of this simple act of forgiveness. If we all based our love on our children's behavior, it would often be difficult to love them at all. If love were based purely on behavior, then perhaps none of us would ever have been loved as a teenager!

Wouldn't it be nice if we could try to extend this same loving-kindness toward everyone we meet? Wouldn't we live in a more loving world if, when someone acted in a way that we didn't approve of, we could see their actions in a similar light as our teenagers' offbeat behavior?

This doesn't mean that we walk around with our heads in the sand, pretend that everything is always wonderful, allow others to "walk all over us," or that we excuse or approve of negative behavior. Instead, it simply means having the perspective to give others the benefit of the doubt. Know that when the postal clerk is moving slowly, he is probably having a bad day, or perhaps all of his days are bad. When your spouse or close friend snaps at you, try to understand that, beneath this isolated act, your loved one really wants to love you, and to feel loved by you. Looking beyond behavior is easier than you might think. Try it today, and you'll see and feel some nice results.

36.

See the Innocence

For many people, one of the most frustrating aspects of life is not being able to understand other people's behavior. We see them as "guilty" instead of "innocent." It's tempting to focus on people's seemingly irrational behavior—their comments, actions, mean-spirited acts, selfish behavior—and get extremely frustrated. If we focus on behavior too much, it can seem like other people are making us miserable.

But as I once heard Wayne Dyer sarcastically suggest in a lecture, "Round up all the people who are making you miserable and bring them to me. I will treat them [as a counselor], and you'll get better!" Obviously, this is absurd. It's true that other people do weird things (who doesn't?), but *we* are the ones getting upset, so we are the ones who need to change. I'm not talking about accepting, ignoring, or advocating violence or any other deviant behavior. I'm merely talking about learning to be less *bothered* by the actions of people.

Seeing the innocence is a powerful tool for transformation

that means when someone is acting in a way that we don't like, the best strategy for dealing with that person is to distance ourselves from the behavior; to "look beyond it," so that we can see the innocence in where the behavior is coming from. Very often, this slight shift in our thinking immediately puts us into a state of compassion.

Occasionally, I work with people who are pressuring me to hurry up. Often, their technique for getting me to hurry along is obnoxious, even insulting. If I focus on the words they use, the tone of their voices, and the urgency of their messages, I can get annoyed, even angry in my responses. I see them as "guilty." However, if I remember the urgency *I* feel when I'm in a hurry to do something, it allows me to see the innocence in their behavior. Underneath even the most annoying behavior is a frustrated person who is crying out for compassion.

The next time (and hopefully from now on), when someone acts in a strange way, look for the innocence in his behavior. If you're compassionate, it won't be hard to see. When you see the innocence, the same things that have always frustrated you no longer do. And, when you're not frustrated by the actions of others, it's a lot easier to stay focused on the beauty of life.

37.

Choose Being Kind over Being Right

As I first introduced in strategy number 12, you are given many opportunities to choose between being kind and being right. You have chances to point out to someone their mistakes, things they could or should have done differently, ways they can improve. You have chances to "correct" people, privately as well as in front of others. What all these opportunities amount to are chances to make someone else feel bad, and yourself feel bad in the process.

Without getting too psychoanalytical about it, the reason we are tempted to put others down, correct them, or show them how we're right and they're wrong is that our ego mistakenly believes that if we point out how someone else is wrong, we must be right, and therefore we will feel better.

In actuality, however, if you pay attention to the way you feel after you put someone down, you'll notice that you feel worse than before the put-down. Your heart, the compassionate part of you, knows that it's impossible to feel better at the expense of someone else.

Luckily, the opposite is true—when your goal is to build people up, to make them feel better, to share in their joy, you too reap the rewards of their positive feelings. The next time you have the chance to correct someone, even if their facts are a little off, resist the temptation. Instead, ask yourself, "What do I really want out of this interaction?" Chances are, what you want is a peaceful interaction where all parties leave feeling good. Each time you resist "being right," and instead choose kindness, you'll notice a peaceful feeling within.

Recently my wife and I were discussing a business idea that had turned out really well. I was talking about "my" idea, clearly taking credit for our success! Kris, in her usual loving manner, allowed me to have the glory. Later that day, I remembered that the idea was actually her idea, not mine. Whoops! When I called her to apologize, it was obvious to me that she cared more for my joy than she did her own need to take credit. She said that she enjoys seeing me happy and that it doesn't matter whose idea it was. (Do you see why she's so easy to love?)

Don't confuse this strategy with being a wimp, or not standing up for what you believe in. I'm not suggesting that it's not okay for you to be right—only that if you *insist* on being right, there is often a price to pay—your inner peace. In order to be a person filled with equanimity, you must choose kindness over being right, most of the time. The best place to start is with the next person you speak to.

38.

Tell Three People (Today) How Much
You Love Them

Author Stephen Levine asks the question, "If you had an hour to live and could make only one phone call—who would you call, what would you say, and why are you waiting?" What a powerful message!

Who knows what we are waiting for? Perhaps we want to believe we will live forever, or that "someday" we will get around to telling the people we love how much we love them. Whatever the reasons, most of us simply wait too long.

As fate would have it, I'm writing this strategy on my grandmother's birthday. Later today, my father and I are driving out to visit her grave site. She died about two years ago. Before she passed away, it became obvious how important it was to her to let her family know how much she loved us all. It was a good reminder that there is no good reason to wait. Now is the time to let people know how much you care.

Ideally, you can tell someone in person or over the phone. I wonder how many people have been on the receiving end of a phone call where the caller says, "I just called to tell you how much I love you!" You may be surprised that almost nothing in the world means so much to a person. How would you like to receive the same message?

If you're too shy to make such a phone call, write a heartfelt letter instead. Either way, you may find that as you get used to it, letting people know how much you love them will become a regular part of your life. It probably won't shock you to know that, if it does, you'll probably begin receiving more love as a result.

39.

Practice Humility

Humility and inner peace go hand in hand. The less compelled you are to try to prove yourself to others, the easier it is to feel peaceful inside.

Proving yourself is a dangerous trap. It takes an enormous amount of energy to be continually pointing out your accomplishments, bragging, or trying to convince others of your worth as a human being. Bragging actually dilutes the positive feelings you receive from an accomplishment or something you are proud of. To make matters worse, the more you try to prove yourself, the more others will avoid you, talk behind your back about your insecure need to brag, and perhaps even resent you.

Ironically, however, the less you care about seeking approval, the more approval you seem to get. People are drawn to those with a quiet, inner confidence, people who don't need to *make* themselves look good, be "right" all the time, or steal the glory. Most people love a person who doesn't need to brag, a person who shares from his or her heart and not from his or her ego.

The way to develop genuine humility is to practice. It's nice because you will get immediate inner feedback in the way of calm, easy feelings. The next time you have an opportunity to brag, resist the temptation. I discussed this strategy with a client, and he shared the following story: He was with a group of friends a few days after he had been promoted at work. His friends didn't know it yet, but my client was chosen to be promoted instead of another friend of theirs. He was a little competitive with this person, and had the very strong temptation to sneak in the fact that he had been chosen and their other friend *wasn't*. He felt himself about ready to say something, when a little voice inside him said, "Stop. Don't do it!" He went ahead and shared with his friends, but didn't cross the line and turn the sharing into gloating. He never mentioned how their other friend didn't get promoted. He told me that he couldn't remember ever feeling so calm and proud of himself. He was able to enjoy his success without bragging. Later, when his friends did find out what had happened, they let him know that they were extremely impressed with his good judgment and humility. He received more positive feedback and attention from practicing humility—not less.

40.

When in Doubt about Whose Turn It Is
to Take Out the Trash,
Go Ahead and Take It Out

If we're not careful, it's easy to become resentful about all the responsibilities of daily living. Once, in a very low mood, I figured out that on an average day, I do over 1,000 different things. Of course, when I'm in a better mood, that number is significantly lower.

As I think about it, it's astounding to me how easy it is for me to remember all the chores that I do, as well as all the other responsibilities that I take care of. But, at the same time, it's easy for me to forget all the things that my wife does on a daily basis. How convenient!

It's really difficult to become a contented person if you're keeping score of all you do. Keeping track only discourages you by cluttering your mind with who's doing what, who's doing more, and so forth. If you want to know the truth about it, this is the epitome of "small stuff." It will bring you far more joy to your life to know that you have done your part and someone else in your family has one less thing to do, than it will to worry and fret over whose turn it is to take out the trash.

The strongest argument against this strategy is the concern that you'll be taken advantage of. This mistake is similar to believing it's important that you're right. Most of the time it's *not* important that you're right, and neither is it important if you take the trash out a few more times than your spouse or housemate. Making things like garbage less relevant in your life will undoubtedly free up more time and energy for truly important things.

41.

Avoid Weatherproofing

The idea of weatherproofing as it pertains to peaceful living is a metaphor to explain one of our most neurotic, ungrateful tendencies. It comes from a friend of mine, Dr. George Pransky.

Just as we can weatherproof a home for the winter by looking for cracks, leaks, and imperfections, we can also weatherproof our relationships, even our lives, by doing the very same thing. Essentially, weatherproofing means that you are on the careful lookout for what needs to be fixed or repaired. It's finding the cracks and flaws of life, and either trying to fix them, or at least point them out to others. Not only does this tendency alienate you from other people, it makes you feel bad, too. It encourages you to think about what's *wrong* with everything and everyone—what you don't like. So, rather than appreciating our relationships and our lives, weatherproofing encourages us to end up thinking that life isn't all it's cracked up to be. Nothing is ever good enough the way it is.

In our relationships, weatherproofing typically plays itself out like this: You meet someone and all is well. You are attracted to his or her appearance, personality, intellect, sense of humor, or some combination of these traits. Initially, you not only approve of your differences with this person, you actually appreciate them. You might even be attracted to the person, in part because of how different you are. You have different opinions, preferences, tastes, and priorities.

After a while, however, you begin to notice little quirks about your new partner (or friend, teacher, whoever), that you feel could be improved upon. You bring it to their attention. You might say, "You know, you sure have a tendency to be late." Or, "I've noticed you don't read very much." The point is, you've begun what inevitably turns into a way of life—looking for and thinking about what you *don't like* about someone, or something that isn't quite right.

Obviously, an occasional comment, constructive criticism, or helpful guidance isn't cause for alarm. I have to say, however, that in the course of working with hundreds of couples over the years, I've met very few people who didn't feel that they were weatherproofed at times by their partner. Occasional harmless comments have an insidious tendency to become a way of looking at life.

When you are weatherproofing another human being, it says

nothing about them—but it does define you as someone who needs to be critical.

Whether you have a tendency to weatherproof your relationships, certain aspects of your life, or both, what you need to do is write off weatherproofing as a bad idea. As the habit creeps into your thinking, catch yourself and seal your lips. The less often you weatherproof your partner or your friends, the more you'll notice how super your life really is.

42.

Spend a Moment, Every Day,
Thinking of Someone to Love

Earlier in this book I introduced the idea of spending a moment, each day, thinking of someone to thank. Another excellent source of gratitude and inner peace is to spend a moment, every day, thinking of someone to love. Remember the old saying, "An apple a day keeps the doctor away?" The love equivalent might read, "Thinking of someone to love each day keeps your resentment away!"

I started consciously choosing to think of people to love when I realized how often I could get caught up in thinking about the opposite—people who irritate me. My mind would focus on negative or strange behavior, and within seconds I was filled with negativity. Once I made the conscious decision, however, to spend a moment each morning thinking of someone to love, my attention was redirected toward the positive, not only toward that one person, but in general throughout the day. I don't mean to suggest that I never get irritated anymore, but without question it happens much less frequently than it used to. I credit this exercise with much of my improvement.

Every morning when I wake up, I close my eyes and take a few deep breaths. Then I ask myself the question, "Who shall I send love to today?" Instantly, a picture of someone will pop into my mind—a family member, a friend, someone I work with, a neighbor, someone from my past, even a stranger I may have seen on the street. To me, it doesn't really matter who it is because the idea is to gear my mind toward love. Once the person to whom I'm directing the love is clear, I simply wish them a day filled with love. I might say to myself something like, "I hope you have a wonderful day filled with loving kindness." When I'm finished, which is within seconds, I usually feel that my heart is ready to begin my day. In some mystical way that I can't explain, those few seconds stick with me for many hours. If you give this little exercise a try, I think you'll find that your day is a little more peaceful.

43.

Become an Anthropologist

Anthropology is a science dealing with man and his origins. In this strategy, however, I'll conveniently redefine anthropology as "being interested, without judgment, in the way other people choose to live and behave." This strategy is geared toward developing your compassion, as well as a way of becoming more patient. Beyond that, however, being interested in the way other people act is a way of replacing judgments with loving-kindness. When you are genuinely curious about the way someone reacts or the way they feel about something, it's unlikely that you will also be annoyed. In this way, becoming an anthropologist is a way of becoming less frustrated by the actions of others.

When someone acts in a way that seems strange to you, rather than reacting in your usual way, such as, "I can't believe they would do that," instead say something to yourself like "I see, that must be the way she sees things in her world. Very interesting." In order for this strategy to help you, you have to be genuine. There's a fine line between being "interested" and being arrogant, as if secretly you believe that your way is better.

Recently I was at a local shopping mall with my six-year-old daughter. A group of punk rockers walked by with orange spiked hair and tattoos covering much of their bodies. My daughter immediately asked me, "Daddy, why are they dressed up like that? Are they in costumes?" Years ago I would have felt very judgmental and frustrated about these young people—as if their way was wrong and my more conservative way was right. I would have blurted out some judgmental explanation to my daughter and passed along to her my judgmental views. Pretending to be an anthropologist, however, has changed my perspective a great deal; it's made me softer. I said to my daughter, "I'm not really sure, but it's interesting how different we all are, isn't it?" She said, "Yeah, but I like my own hair." Rather than focusing on the behavior and continuing to give it energy, we both dropped it and continued to enjoy our time together.

When you are interested in other perspectives, it doesn't imply, even slightly, that you're advocating it. I certainly wouldn't choose a punk rock lifestyle or suggest it to anyone else. At the same time, however, it's really not my place to judge it either. One of the cardinal rules of joyful living is that judging others takes a great deal of energy and, without exception, pulls you away from where you want to be.

44.

Understand Separate Realities

While we're on the subject of being interested in the way other people do things, let's take a moment to discuss separate realities.

If you have traveled to foreign countries or seen depictions of them in movies, you are aware of vast differences among cultures. The principle of separate realities says that the differences among individuals is every bit as vast. Just as we wouldn't expect people of different cultures to see or do things as we would (in fact, we'd be disappointed if they did), this principle tells us that the individual differences in our ways of seeing the world prohibit this as well. It's not a matter of merely tolerating differences but of truly understanding and honoring the fact that it literally can't be any other way.

I have seen an understanding of this principle change lives. It can virtually eliminate quarrels. When we expect to see things differently, when we take it as a given that others will do things differently and react differently to the same stimuli, the compassion we have for ourselves and for others rises dramatically. The moment we expect otherwise, the potential for conflict exists.

I encourage you to consider deeply and respect the fact that we are all very different. When you do, the love you feel for others as well as the appreciation you have for your own uniqueness will increase.

45.

Develop Your Own Helping Rituals

I f you want your life to stand for peace and kindness, it's helpful to do kind, peaceful things. One of my favorite ways to do this is by developing my own helping rituals. These little acts of kindness are opportunities to be of service and reminders of how good it feels to be kind and helpful.

We live in a rural area of the San Francisco Bay Area. Most of what we see is beauty and nature. One of the exceptions to the beauty is the litter that some people throw out of their windows as they are driving on the rural roads. One of the few drawbacks to living out in the boondocks is that public services, such as litter collection, are less available than they are closer to the city.

A helping ritual that I practice regularly with my two children is picking up litter in our surrounding area. We've become so accustomed to doing this that my daughters will often say to me in animated voices, "There's some litter, Daddy, stop the car!" And if we have time, we will often pull over and pick it up. It may seem strange, but we actually enjoy it. We pick up litter in parks, on sidewalks, practically anywhere. Once I even saw a complete stranger picking up litter close to where we live. He smiled at me and said, "I saw you doing it, and it seemed like a good idea."

Picking up litter is only one of an endless supply of possible helping rituals. You might like holding a door open for people, visiting lonely elderly people in nursing homes, or shoveling snow off someone else's driveway. Think of something that seems effortless yet helpful. It's fun, personally rewarding, and sets a good example. Everyone wins.

46.

Every Day, Tell at Least One Person Something You Like, Admire, or Appreciate about Them

How often do you remember (or take the time), to tell people how much you like, admire, or appreciate them? For many people, it's not often enough. In fact, when I ask people how often they *receive* heartfelt compliments from others, I hear answers like "I can't remember the last time I received a compliment," "Hardly ever," and, sadly, "I never receive them."

There are several reasons why we don't vocally let others know about our positive feelings toward them. I've heard excuses like, "They don't need to hear me say that—they already know," and "I do admire her, but I'm too embarrassed to say anything." But when you ask the would-be recipient if he or she enjoys being given genuine compliments and positive feedback, the answer nine times out of ten is, "I love it." Whether your reason for *not* giving compliments on a regular basis is not knowing what to say, embarrassment, feeling that other people already know their strengths and don't need to be told, or simply not being in the habit of doing it, it's time for a change.

Telling someone something that you like, admire, or appreciate about them is a "random act of kindness." It takes almost no effort (once you get used to it), yet it pays enormous dividends. Many people spend their entire lifetimes wishing that other people would acknowledge them. They feel this especially about their parents, spouses, children, and friends. But even compliments from strangers feel good if they are genuine. Letting someone know how you feel about them also feels good to the person offering the compliment. It's a gesture of loving-kindness. It means that your thoughts are geared toward what's right with someone. And when your thoughts are geared in a positive direction, your feelings are peaceful.

The other day I was in the grocery store and witnessed an incredible display of patience. The checkout clerk had just been chewed out by an angry customer, clearly without good cause. Rather than being reactive, the clerk defused the anger by remaining calm. When it was my turn to pay for my groceries I said to her, "I'm so impressed at the way you handled that customer." She looked me right in the eye and said, "Thank you, sir. Do you know you are the first person ever to give me a compliment in this store?" It took less than two seconds to let her know, yet it was a highlight of her day, and of mine.

47.

Argue for Your Limitations,
and They're Yours

Many people spend a great deal of energy arguing for their own limitations; "I can't do that," "I can't help it, I've always been that way," "I'll never have a loving relationship," and thousands of other negative and self-defeating statements.

Our minds are powerful instruments. When we decide that something is true or beyond our reach, it's very difficult to pierce through this self-created hurdle. When we argue for our position, it's nearly impossible. Suppose, for example, you tell yourself, "I can't write." You'll look for examples to prove your position. You'll remember your poor essays in high school, or recall how awkward you felt the last time you sat down to write a letter. You'll fill your head with limitations that will frighten you from trying. In order to become a writer or anything else, the first step is to silence your greatest critic—you.

I had a client who told me, "I'll never have a good relationship. I always screw them up." Sure enough, she was right. Whenever she met someone, she would, without even knowing it, look for reasons for her new partner to leave her. If she were late for a date, she would tell him, "I'm always late." If they had a disagreement, she would say, "I'm always getting into arguments." Sooner or later, she would convince him that she wasn't worthy of his love. Then she would say to herself, "See, it happens every time. I'll never have a good relationship."

She had to learn to stop expecting things to go wrong. She needed to "catch herself" in the act of arguing for her own limitations. When she started to say, "I always do that," she needed instead to say, "That's ridiculous. I don't *always* do anything." She had to see that arguing for her limitations was just a negative habit that could easily be replaced with a more positive habit. Today, she's doing much better. When she reverts to her old habit, she usually laughs at herself.

I have learned that when I argue for my own limitations, very seldom do I disappoint myself. I suspect the same is true for you.

48.

Remember that Everything Has God's Fingerprints on It

Rabbi Harold Kushner reminds us that everything that God has created is potentially holy. Our task as humans is to find that holiness in what appear to be unholy situations. He suggests that when we can learn to do this, we will have learned to nurture our souls. It's easy to see God's beauty in a beautiful sunrise, a snow-capped mountain, the smile of a healthy child, or in ocean waves crashing on a sandy beach. But can we learn to find the holiness in seemingly ugly circumstances—difficult life lessons, a family tragedy, or a struggle for life?

When our life is filled with the desire to see the holiness in everyday things, something magical begins to happen. A feeling of peace emerges. We begin to see nurturing aspects of daily living that were previously hidden to us. When we remember that everything has God's fingerprints on it, that alone makes it special. If we remember this spiritual fact while we are dealing with a difficult person or struggling to pay our bills, it broadens our perspective. It helps us to remember that God also created the person you are dealing with or that, despite your struggle to pay your bills, you are truly blessed to have all that you do.

Somewhere, in the back of your mind, try to remember that everything has God's fingerprints on it. The fact that we can't see the beauty in something doesn't suggest that it's not there. Rather, it suggests that we are not looking carefully enough or with a broad enough perspective to see it.

49.

Resist the Urge to Criticize

When we judge or criticize another person, it says nothing about that person; it merely says something about our own need to be critical.

If you attend a gathering and listen to all the criticism that is typically levied against others, and then go home and consider how much good all that criticism actually does to make our world a better place, you'll probably come up with the same answer that I do: Zero! It does no good. But that's not all. Being critical not only solves nothing; it contributes to the anger and distrust in our world. After all, none of us likes to be criticized. Our reaction to criticism is usually to become defensive and/or withdrawn. A person who feels attacked is likely to do one of two things: he will either retreat in fear or shame, or he will attack or lash out in anger. How many times have you criticized someone and had them respond by saying, "Thank you so much for pointing out my flaws. I really appreciate it"?

Criticism, like swearing, is actually nothing more than a bad habit. It's something we get used to doing; we're familiar with how it feels. It keeps us busy and gives us something to talk about.

If, however, you take a moment to observe how you actually feel immediately after you criticize someone, you'll notice that you will feel a little deflated and ashamed, almost like *you're* the one who has been attacked. The reason this is true is that when we criticize, it's a statement to the world and to ourselves, "I have a need to be critical." This isn't something we are usually proud to admit.

The solution is to catch yourself in the act of being critical. Notice how often you do it and how bad it makes you feel. What I like to do is turn it into a game. I still catch myself being critical, but as my need to criticize arises, I try to remember to say to myself, "There I go again." Hopefully, more often than not, I can turn my criticism into tolerance and respect.

50.

Write Down Your Five Most Stubborn Positions and See if You Can Soften Them

The first time I tried this strategy, I was so stubborn that I insisted that I *wasn't* stubborn! Over time, as I have worked toward becoming a gentler person, I have found it far easier to see where I'm being stubborn.

Here are a few examples from my clients: "People who aren't stressed are lazy." "My way is the only way." "Men aren't good listeners." "Women spend too much money." "Children are too much work." "People in business don't care about anything except money." You can see that the list itself is potentially endless. The point here isn't the specifics of what you are stubborn about but rather the fact that you hold on so tightly to any given idea you might have.

It doesn't make you weak to soften your positions. In fact, it makes you stronger. I have a male client who was adamant, to the point of being obnoxious about it, that his wife spent too much money. As he relaxed a little, and noticed his own rigidity, he discovered something that he's now a little embarrassed about, but laughs at. He found out that, in reality, he spent *more* discretionary money on himself than his wife spent on herself! His objectivity had become muddled by his own rigid belief.

As he has become wiser and gentler, his marriage has improved immensely. Rather than resenting his wife for something she wasn't even doing, he now appreciates her restraint. She, in turn, feels his new acceptance and appreciation and loves him more than before.

51.

Just for Fun, Agree with Criticism Directed Toward You (Then Watch It Go Away)

So often we are immobilized by the slightest criticism. We treat it like an emergency, and defend ourselves as if we were in a battle. In truth, however, criticism is nothing more than an observation by another person about us, our actions, or the way we think about something, that doesn't match the vision we have of ourselves. Big deal!

When we react to criticism with a knee-jerk, defensive response, it hurts. We feel attacked, and we have a need to defend or to offer a countercriticism. We fill our minds with angry or hurtful thoughts directed at ourselves or at the person who is being critical. All this reaction takes an enormous amount of mental energy.

An incredibly useful exercise is to agree with criticism directed toward you. I'm not talking about turning into a doormat or ruining your self-esteem by believing all negativity that comes in your direction. I'm only suggesting that there are many times when simply agreeing with criticism defuses the situation, satisfies a person's need to express a point of view, offers you a chance to learn something about yourself by seeing a grain of truth in another position, and, perhaps most important, provides you an opportunity to remain calm.

One of the first times I consciously agreed with criticism directed toward me was many years ago when my wife said to me, "Sometimes you talk too much." I remember feeling momentarily hurt before deciding to agree. I responded by saying, "You're right, I do talk too much sometimes." I discovered something that changed my life. In agreeing with her, I was able to see that she had a good point. I often do talk too much! What's more, my nondefensive reaction helped her to relax. A few minutes later she said, "You know, you're sure easy to talk to." I doubt she would have said that had I become angry at her observation. I've since learned that reacting to criticism never makes the criticism go away. In fact, negative reactions to criticism often convince the person doing the criticizing that they are accurate in their assessment of you.

Give this strategy a try. I think you'll discover that agreeing with an occasional criticism has more value than it costs.

52.

Search for the Grain of Truth
in Other Opinions

I f you enjoy learning as well as making other people happy, you'll love this idea.

Almost everyone feels that their own opinions are good ones, otherwise they wouldn't be sharing them with you. One of the destructive things that many of us do, however, is compare someone else's opinion to our own. And, when it doesn't fall in line with our belief, we either dismiss it or find fault with it. We feel smug, the other person feels diminished, and we learn nothing.

Almost every opinion has some merit, especially if we are looking for merit, rather than looking for errors. The next time someone offers you an opinion, rather than judge or criticize it, see if you can find a grain of truth in what the person is saying.

If you think about it, when you judge someone else or their opinion, it really doesn't say *anything* about the other person, but it says quite a bit about your need to be judgmental.

I still catch myself criticizing other points of view, but far less than I used to. All that changed was my intention to find the grain of truth in other positions. If you practice this simple strategy, some wonderful things will begin to happen: You'll begin to understand those you interact with, others will be drawn to your accepting and loving energy, your learning curve will be enhanced, and, perhaps most important, you'll feel much better about yourself.

53.

See the Glass as Already Broken
(and Everything Else Too)

This is a Buddhist teaching that I learned over twenty years ago. It has provided me, again and again, with greatly needed perspective to guide me toward my goal of a more accepting self.

The essence of this teaching is that all of life is in a constant state of change. Everything has a beginning and everything has an end. Every tree begins with a seed and will eventually transform back into earth. Every rock is formed and every rock will vanish. In our modern world, this means that every car, every machine, every piece of clothing is created and all will wear out and crumble; it's only a matter of when. Our bodies are born and they will die. A glass is created and will eventually break.

There is peace to be found in this teaching. When you expect something to break, you're not surprised or disappointed when it does. Instead of becoming immobilized when something is destroyed, you feel grateful for the time you have had.

The easiest place to start is with the simple things, a glass of water, for example. Pull out your favorite drinking glass. Take a moment to look at and appreciate its beauty and all it does for you. Now, imagine that same glass as already broken, shattered all over the floor. Try to maintain the perspective that, in time, everything disintegrates and returns to its initial form.

Obviously, no one wants their favorite drinking glass, or anything else, to be broken. This philosophy is not a prescription for becoming passive or apathetic, but for making peace with the way things are. When your drinking glass does break, this philosophy allows you to maintain your perspective. Rather than thinking, "Oh my God," you'll find yourself thinking, "Ah, there it goes." Play with this awareness and you'll find yourself not only keeping your cool but appreciating life as never before.

54.

Understand the Statement,

"Wherever You Go, There You Are"

This is the title of a super book by Jon Kabat-Zinn. As the title suggests, wherever you go, you take yourself with you! The significance of this statement is that it can teach you to stop constantly wishing you were somewhere else. We tend to believe that if we were somewhere else—on vacation, with another partner, in a different career, a different home, a different circumstance—somehow we would be happier and more content. We wouldn't!

The truth is, if you have destructive mental habits—if you get annoyed and bothered easily, if you feel angry and frustrated a great deal of the time, or if you're constantly wishing things were different, these identical tendencies will follow you, wherever you go. And the reverse is also true. If you are a generally happy person who rarely gets annoyed and bothered, then you can move from place to place, from person to person, with very little negative impact.

Someone once asked me, "What are the people like in California?" I asked him, "What are the people like in your home state?" He replied, "Selfish and greedy." I told him that he would probably find the people in California to be selfish and greedy.

Something wonderful begins to happen with the simple realization that life, like an automobile, is driven from the inside out, not the other way around. As you focus more on becoming more peaceful with where you are, rather than focusing on where you would *rather* be, you begin to find peace right now, in the present. Then, as you move around, try new things, and meet new people, you carry that sense of inner peace with you. It's absolutely true that "Wherever you go, there you are."

55.

Breathe Before You Speak

This simple strategy has had remarkable results for virtually everyone I know who has tried it. The almost immediate results include increased patience, added perspective, and, as a side benefit, more gratitude and respect from others.

The strategy itself is remarkably simple. It involves nothing more than pausing—breathing—after the person to whom you are speaking is finished. At first, the time gap between your voices may seem like an eternity—but in reality, it amounts to only a fraction of a second of actual time. You will get used to the power and beauty of breathing, and you will come to appreciate it as well. It will bring you closer to, and earn you more respect from, virtually everyone you come in contact with. You'll find that being listened to is one of the rarest and most treasured gifts you can offer. All it takes is intention and practice.

If you observe the conversations around you, you'll notice

that, often, what many of us do is simply wait for *our* chance to speak. We're not *really* listening to the other person, but simply waiting for an opening to express our own view. We often complete other people's sentences, or say things like, "Yeah, yeah," or "I know," very rapidly, urging them to hurry up so that we can have our turn. It seems that talking to one another is sometimes more like sparring back and forth like fighters or Ping-Pong balls than it is enjoying or learning from the conversation.

This harried form of communication encourages us to criticize points of view, overreact, misinterpret meaning, impute false motives, and form opinions, all before our fellow communicator is even finished speaking. No wonder we are so often annoyed, bothered, and irritated with one another. Sometimes, with our poor listening skills, it's a miracle that we have any friends at all!

I spent most of my life waiting for my turn to speak. If you're at all like me, you'll be pleasantly amazed at the softer reactions and looks of surprise as you let others completely finish their thought before you begin yours. Often, you will be allowing someone to feel listened to for the very first time. You will sense a feeling of relief coming from the person to whom you are speaking—and a much calmer, less rushed feeling between the two of you. No need to worry that you won't get your turn to speak—you will. In fact, it will be more rewarding to speak because the person you are speaking to will pick up on your respect and patience and will begin to do the same.

56.

Be Grateful when You're Feeling Good and Graceful when You're Feeling Bad

The happiest person on earth isn't always happy. In fact, the happiest people *all* have their fair share of low moods, problems, disappointments, and heartache. Often the difference between a person who is happy and someone who is unhappy isn't how often they get low, or even how low they drop, but instead, it's what they do with their low moods. How do they relate to their changing feelings?

Most people have it backward. When they are feeling down, they roll up their sleeves and get to work. They take their low moods very seriously and try to figure out and analyze what's wrong. They try to force themselves out of their low state, which tends to compound the problem rather than solve it.

When you observe peaceful, relaxed people, you find that when they are feeling good, they are very grateful. They understand that both positive and negative feelings come and go, and that there will come a time when they won't be feeling so good. To happy people, this is okay, it's the way of things. They accept the inevitability of passing feelings. So, when they are feeling depressed, angry, or stressed out, they relate to these feelings with the same openness and wisdom. Rather than fight their feelings and panic simply because they are feeling bad, they accept their feelings, knowing that this too shall pass. Rather than stumbling and fighting against their negative feelings, they are graceful in their acceptance of them. This allows them to come gently and gracefully out of negative feeling states into more positive states of mind. One of the happiest people I know is someone who also gets quite low from time to time. The difference, it seems, is that he has become comfortable with his low moods. It's almost as though he doesn't really care because he knows that, in due time, he will be happy again. To him, it's no big deal.

The next time you're feeling bad, rather than fight it, try to relax. See if, instead of panicking, you can be graceful and calm. Know that if you don't fight your negative feelings, if you are graceful, they will pass away just as surely as the sun sets in the evening.

57.

Become a Less Aggressive Driver

Where do you get the most uptight? If you're like most people, driving in traffic is probably high on your list. To look at most major freeways these days, you'd think you were on a racetrack instead of a roadway.

There are three excellent reasons for becoming a less aggressive driver. First, when you are aggressive, you put yourself and everyone around you in extreme danger. Second, driving aggressively is extremely stressful. Your blood pressure goes up, your grip on the wheel tightens, your eyes are strained, and your thoughts are spinning out of control. Finally, you end up saving no time in getting to where you want to go.

Recently I was driving south from Oakland to San Jose. Traffic was heavy, but moving. I noticed an extremely aggressive and angry driver weaving in and out of the lanes, speeding up and slowing down. Clearly, he was in a hurry. For the most part I remained in the same lane for the entire forty-mile journey. I was listening to a new audiotape I had just purchased and day-dreaming along the way. I enjoyed the trip a great deal because driving gives me a chance to be alone. As I was exiting off the freeway, the aggressive driver came up behind me and raced on by. Without realizing it, I had actually arrived in San Jose ahead of him. All of his weaving, rapid acceleration, and putting families at risk had earned him nothing except perhaps some high blood pressure and a great deal of wear and tear on his vehicle. On average, he and I had driven at the same speed.

The same principle applies when you see drivers speeding past you so that they can beat you to the next stoplight. It simply doesn't pay to speed. This is especially true if you get a ticket and have to spend eight hours in traffic school. It will take you years of dangerous speeding to make up this time alone.

When you make the conscious decision to become a less aggressive driver, you begin using your time in the car to relax. Try to see your driving not only as a way of getting you somewhere, but as a chance to breathe and to reflect. Rather than tensing your muscles, see if you can relax them instead. I even have a few audiotapes that are specifically geared toward muscular relaxation. Sometimes I pop one in and listen. By the time I reach my destination I feel more relaxed than I did before getting into the car. During the course of your lifetime, you're probably going to spend a great deal of time driving. You can spend those moments being frustrated, or you can use them wisely. If you do the latter, you'll be a more relaxed person.

58.

Relax

What does it mean to relax? Despite hearing this term thousands of times during the course of our lives, very few people have deeply considered what it's really about.

When you ask people (which I have done many times) what it means to relax, most will answer in a way that suggests that relaxing is something you plan to do later—you do it on vacation, in a hammock, when you retire, or when you get everything done. This implies, of course, that most other times (the other 95 percent of your life) should be spent nervous, agitated, rushed, and frenzied. Very few actually come out and say so, but this is the obvious implication. Could this explain why so many of us operate as if life were one great big emergency? Most of us postpone relaxation until our "in basket" is empty. Of course it never is.

It's useful to think of relaxation as a quality of heart that you can access on a regular basis rather than something reserved for some later time. You can relax now. It's helpful to remember that relaxed people can still be superachievers and, in fact, that relaxation and creativity go hand in hand. When I'm feeling uptight, for example, I don't even try to write. But when I feel relaxed, my writing flows quickly and easily.

Being more relaxed involves training yourself to respond differently to the dramas of life—turning your melodrama into a mellow-drama. It comes, in part, from reminding yourself over and over again (with loving kindness and patience) that you have a choice in how you respond to life. You can learn to relate to your thinking as well as your circumstances in new ways. With practice, making these choices will translate into a more relaxed self.

59.

Adopt a Child Through the Mail

While I don't want to turn this book into an advertisement for service agencies, I do have to say that my experience of adopting children through the mail has been extremely positive. No, you don't actually *adopt* a child, but you do get to help one out while, at the same time, getting to know them. The experience has brought tremendous joy and satisfaction to my entire family. My six-year-old daughter has an adoptee, and has enjoyed and learned from the experience a great deal. My daughter and her pal regularly write to each other, and draw pictures that we hang up. They enjoy hearing about each other's lives.

Each month you contribute a very small amount of money to the agency in charge of helping the children. The money is used to help the children and their parents with the necessities of life, which makes sending the children to school and caring for their needs a little easier.

I think that the reason we enjoy this type of giving so much is that it's interactive. So often, when you give to a charity, you have no way of knowing who you are helping. In this instance, you not only get to know who, but you have the privilege of getting to know them as well. Also, the regularity of the ongoing relationship reminds you how fortunate you are to be in a position to help. For me and for many people that I know, this type of giving brings forth feelings of gratitude. There are many fine agencies to choose from, but my personal favorite is Children, Inc., out of Richmond, Virginia, (800) 538-5381.

60.

Turn Your Melodrama into a Mellow-Drama

In a certain respect, this strategy is just another way of saying, "Don't sweat the small stuff." Many people live as if life were a melodrama—"an extravagantly theatrical play in which action and plot predominate." Sound familiar? In dramatic fashion, we blow things out of proportion, and make a big deal out of little things. We forget that life isn't as bad as we're making it out to be. We also forget that when we're blowing things out of proportion, *we* are the ones doing the blowing.

I've found that simply reminding myself that life doesn't have to be a soap opera is a powerful method of calming down. When I get too worked up or start taking myself too seriously (which happens more than I like to admit), I say to myself something like, "Here I go again. My soap opera is starting." Almost always, this takes the edge off my seriousness and helps me laugh at myself. Often, this simple reminder enables me to change the channel to a more peaceful station. My melodrama is transformed into a "mellow-drama."

If you've ever watched a soap opera, you've seen how the characters will take little things so seriously as to ruin their lives over them—someone says something to offend them, looks at them wrong, or flirts with their spouse. Their response is usually, "Oh my gosh. How could this happen to me?" Then they exacerbate the problem by talking to others about "how awful it is." They turn life into an emergency—a melodrama.

The next time you feel stressed out, experiment with this strategy—remind yourself that life isn't an emergency and turn your melodrama into a mellow-drama.

61.

Read Articles and Books with Entirely Different Points of View from Your Own and Try to Learn Something

Have you ever noticed that practically everything you read justifies and reinforces your own opinions and views on life? The same is true with our radio and television listening and viewing choices as well. In fact, on America's most popular radio talk show, callers often identify themselves as "ditto heads," meaning "I already agree with everything you say. Tell me more." Liberals, conservatives—we're all the same. We form opinions and then spend our entire lifetimes validating what we believe to be true. This rigidity is sad, because there is so much we can learn from points of view that are different from our own. It's also sad because the stubbornness it takes to keep our heart and mind closed to everything other than our own point of view creates a great deal of inner stress. A closed mind is always fighting to keep everything else at arm's length.

We forget that we're all equally convinced that our way of

looking at the world is the only correct way. We forget that two people who disagree with one another can often use the *identical* examples to prove their own point of view—and both sides can be articulate and convincing.

Knowing this, we can either buckle down and get even more stubborn—or we can lighten up and try to learn something new! For just a few minutes a day—whatever your slant on life—try making a gentle effort to read articles and/or books with different points of view. You don't need to change your core beliefs or your deepest held positions. All you're doing is expanding your mind and opening your heart to new ideas. This new openness will reduce the stress it takes to keep other points of view away. In addition to being very interesting, this practice helps you see the innocence in others as well as helping you become more patient. You'll become a more relaxed, philosophic person, because you'll begin to sense the logic in other points of view. My wife and I subscribe to both the most conservative as well as the most liberal newsletters in America. I'd say that both have broadened our perspective on life.

62.

Do One Thing at a Time

The other day I was driving on the freeway and noticed a man who, while driving in the fast lane, was shaving, drinking a cup of coffee, and reading the newspaper! "Perfect," I thought to myself, as just that morning I was trying to think of an appropriate example to point out the craziness of our frenzied society.

How often do we try to do more than one thing at once? We have cordless phones that are supposed to make our lives easier, but in some respects, they make our lives more confusing. My wife and I were at a friend's home for dinner a while ago and noticed her talking on the phone while simultaneously answering the door, checking on dinner, and changing her daughter's diaper (after she washed her hands, of course)! Many of us have the same tendency when we're speaking to someone and our mind is somewhere else, or when we're doing three or four chores all at the same time.

When you do too many things at once, it's impossible to

be present-moment oriented. Thus, you not only lose out on much of the potential enjoyment of what you are doing, but you also become far less focused and effective.

An interesting exercise is to block out periods of time where you commit to doing only one thing at a time. Whether you're washing dishes, talking on the phone, driving a car, playing with your child, talking to your spouse, or reading a magazine, try to focus only on that one thing. Be present in what you are doing. Concentrate. You'll notice two things beginning to happen. First, you'll actually enjoy what you are doing, even something mundane like washing dishes or cleaning out a closet. When you're focused, rather than distracted, it enables you to become absorbed and interested in your activity, whatever it might be. Second, you'll be amazed at how quickly and efficiently you'll get things done. Since I've become more present-moment oriented, my skills have increased in virtually all areas of my life—writing, reading, cleaning house, and speaking on the phone. You can do the same thing. It all starts with your decision to do one thing at a time.

63.

Count to Ten

When I was growing up my father used to count out loud to ten when he was angry with my sisters and me. It was a strategy he, and many other parents, used to cool down before deciding what to do next.

I've improved this strategy by incorporating the use of the breath. All you have to do is this: When you feel yourself getting angry, take a long, deep inhalation, and as you do, say the number one to yourself. Then, relax your entire body as you breathe out. Repeat the same process with the number two, all the way through *at least* ten (if you're really angry, continue to twenty-five). What you are doing here is clearing your mind with a mini version of a meditation exercise. The combination of counting and breathing is so relaxing that it's almost impossible to remain angry once you are finished. The increased oxygen in your lungs and the time gap between the moment you became angry and the time you finish the exercise enables you to increase your perspective. It helps make "big stuff" look like "little stuff." The exercise is equally effective in working with stress or frustration. Whenever you feel a little off, give it a try.

The truth is, this exercise is a wonderful way to spend a minute or two whether or not you're angry. I've incorporated this strategy into my daily life simply because it's relaxing and I enjoy it. Often, it helps me to keep from getting angry in the first place.

64.

Practice Being in the "Eye of the Storm"

The eye of the storm is that one specific spot in the center of a twister, hurricane, or tornado that is calm, almost isolated from the frenzy of activity. Everything around the center is violent and turbulent, but the center remains peaceful. How nice it would be if we too could be calm and serene in the midst of chaos—in the eye of the storm.

Surprisingly enough, it's much easier that you might imagine to be in the eye of a "human storm." What it takes is intention and practice. Suppose, for example, that you are going to a family gathering that is going to be chaotic. You can tell yourself that you are going to use the experience as an opportunity to remain calm. You can commit to being the one person in the room who is going to be an example of peace. You can practice breathing. You can practice listening. You can let others be right and enjoy the glory. The point is, you can do it if you set your mind to it.

By starting out with harmless scenarios like family gatherings, cocktail parties, and birthday parties for children, you can build a track record and enjoy some success. You'll notice that by being in the eye of the storm, you will be more present-moment oriented. You'll enjoy yourself more than ever before. Once you have mastered harmless circumstances like these, you can practice on more difficult areas of life—dealing with conflict, hardship, or grief. If you start slowly, have some success, and keep practicing, pretty soon you'll know how to live in the eye of the storm.

65.

Be Flexible with Changes in Your Plans

Once I get something in my mind (a plan), it can be tricky to let go of it and go with the flow. I was taught, and to some degree it's certainly true, that success, or successfully completing a project, requires perseverance. At the same time, however, inflexibility creates an enormous amount of inner stress and is often irritating and insensitive to other people.

I like to do the majority of my writing in the wee hours of the morning. I might have the goal, in this book for example, to complete one or two strategies before anyone else in the house wakes up. But what happens if my four-year-old wakes up early and walks upstairs to see me? My plans have certainly been altered, but how do I react? Or, I might have the goal to go out for a run before going to the office. What happens if I get an emergency call from the office and have to skip my run?

There are countless potential examples for all of us—times when our plans suddenly change, something we thought was going to take place doesn't, someone doesn't do what they said they would do, you make less money than you thought you would, someone changes your plans without your consent, you have less time than previously planned, something unexpected comes up—and on and on it goes. The question to ask yourself is, What's *really* important?

We often use the excuse that it's natural to be frustrated when our plans change. That depends, however, on what your priorities are. Is it more important to stick to some rigid writing schedule or to be available to my four-year-old? Is missing a thirty-minute run worth getting upset over? The more general question is, "What's more important, getting what I want and keeping my plans, or learning to go with the flow?" Clearly, to become a more peaceful person, you must prioritize being flexible over rigidity most of the time (obviously there will be exceptions). I've also found it helpful to *expect* that a certain percentage of plans will change. If I make allowances in my mind for this inevitability, then when it happens I can say, "Here is one of those inevitabilities."

You'll find that if you create the goal to become more flexible, some wonderful things will begin to happen: You'll feel more relaxed, yet you won't sacrifice any productivity. You may even become *more* productive because you won't need to expend so much energy being upset and worried. I've learned to trust that I will keep my deadlines, achieve most of my goals, and honor my responsibilities despite the fact that I may have to alter my plans slightly (or even completely). Finally, the people around you will be more relaxed too. They won't feel like they have to walk around on eggshells if, by some chance, your plans have to change.

66.

Think of What You Have Instead of What You Want

In over a dozen years as a stress consultant, one of the most pervasive and destructive mental tendencies I've seen is that of focusing on what we *want* instead of what we *have*. It doesn't seem to make any difference how much we have; we just keep expanding our list of desires, which guarantees we will remain dissatisfied. The mind-set that says "I'll be happy when this desire is fulfilled" is the same mind-set that will repeat itself once that desire is met.

A friend of ours closed escrow on his new home on a Sunday. The very next time we saw him he was talking about his next house that was going to be even bigger! He isn't alone. Most of us do the very same thing. We want this or that. If we don't get what we want we keep thinking about all that we don't have—and we remain dissatisfied. If we do get what we want, we simply re-create the same thinking in our new circumstances. So, despite getting what we want, we still remain unhappy. Happiness can't be found when we are yearning for new desires.

Luckily, there is a way to be happy. It involves changing the emphasis of our thinking from what we want to what we have. Rather than wishing your spouse were different, try thinking about her wonderful qualities. Instead of complaining about your salary, be grateful that you have a job. Rather than wishing you were able to take a vacation to Hawaii, think of how much fun you have had close to home. The list of possibilities is endless! Each time you notice yourself falling into the "I wish life were different" trap, back off and start over. Take a breath and remember all that you have to be grateful for. When you focus not on what you want, but on what you have, you end up getting more of what you want anyway. If you focus on the good qualities of your spouse, she'll be more loving. If you are grateful for your job rather than complaining about it, you'll do a better job, be more productive, and probably end up getting a raise anyway. If you focus on ways to enjoy yourself around home rather than waiting to enjoy yourself in Hawaii, you'll end up having more fun. If you ever do get to Hawaii, you'll be in the habit of enjoying yourself. And, if by some chance you don't, you'll have a great life anyway.

Make a note to yourself to start thinking more about what you have than what you want. If you do, your life will start appearing much better than before. For perhaps the first time in your life, you'll know what it means to feel satisfied.

67.

Practice Ignoring Your Negative Thoughts

It has been estimated that the average human being has around 50,000 thoughts per day. That's a lot of thoughts. Some of these thoughts are going to be positive and productive. Unfortunately, however, many of them are also going to be negative—angry, fearful, pessimistic, worrisome. Indeed, the important question in terms of becoming more peaceful isn't whether or not you're going to have negative thoughts—you are—it's what you choose to do with the ones that you have.

In a practical sense, you really have only two options when it comes to dealing with negative thoughts. You can analyze your thoughts—ponder, think through, study, think some more—or you can learn to ignore them—dismiss, pay less attention to, not take so seriously. This later option, learning to take your negative thoughts less seriously, is infinitely more effective in terms of learning to be more peaceful.

When you have a thought—any thought—that's all it is, a thought! It can't hurt you without your consent. For example, if you have a thought from your past, "I'm upset because my parents didn't do a very good job," you can get into it, as many do, which will create inner turmoil for you. You can give the thought significance in your mind, and you'll convince yourself that you should indeed be unhappy. Or, you can recognize that your mind is about to create a mental snowball, and you can choose to dismiss the thought. This doesn't mean your childhood wasn't difficult—it may very well have been—but in *this* present moment, you have a choice of which thoughts to pay attention to.

The same mental dynamic applies to thoughts of this morning, even five minutes ago. An argument that happened while you were walking out the door on your way to work is no longer an actual argument, it's a thought in your mind. This dynamic also applies to future-oriented thoughts of this evening, next week, or ten years down the road. You'll find, in all cases, that if you ignore or dismiss a negative thought that fills your mind, a more peaceful feeling is only a moment away. And, in a more peaceful state of mind, your wisdom and common sense will tell you what to do. This strategy takes practice but is well worth the effort.

68.

Be Willing to Learn
from Friends and Family

O ne of the saddest observations I've made centers around how reluctant many of us are to learn from the people closest to us—our parents, spouses, children, and friends. Rather than being open to learning, we close ourselves off out of embarrassment, fear, stubbornness, or pride. It's almost as if we say to ourselves, "I have already learned all that I can [or want to learn] from this person; there is nothing else I can [or need to] learn."

It's sad, because often the people closest to us know us the best. They are sometimes able to see ways in which we are acting in a self-defeating manner and can offer very simple solutions. If we are too proud or stubborn to learn, we lose out on some wonderful, simple ways to improve our lives.

I have tried to remain open to the suggestions of my friends and family. In fact, I have gone so far as to ask certain members of my family and a few of my friends, "What are some of my blind spots?" Not only does this make the person you are asking feel wanted and special, but you end up getting some terrific advice. It's such a simple shortcut for growth, yet almost no one uses it. All it takes is a little courage and humility, and the ability to let go of your ego. This is especially true if you are in the habit of ignoring suggestions, taking them as criticism, or tuning out certain members of your family. Imagine how shocked they will be when you ask them, sincerely, for their advice.

Pick something that you feel the person whom you are asking is qualified to answer. For example, I often ask my father for advice on business. Even if he happens to give me a bit of a lecture, it's well worth it. The advice he gives usually prevents me from having to learn something the hard way.

69.

Be Happy Where You Are

Sadly, many of us continually postpone our happiness—indefinitely. It's not that we consciously set out to do so, but that we keep convincing ourselves, "Someday I'll be happy." We tell ourselves we'll be happy when our bills are paid, when we get out of school, get our first job, a promotion. We convince ourselves that life will be better after we get married, have a baby, then another. Then we are frustrated that the kids aren't old enough—we'll be more content when they are. After that, we're frustrated that we have teenagers to deal with. We will certainly be happy when they are out of that stage. We tell ourselves that our life will be complete when our spouse gets his or her act together, when we get a nicer car, are able to go on a nice vacation, when we retire. And on and on and on!

Meanwhile, life keeps moving forward. The truth is, there's no better time to be happy than right now. If not now, when? Your life will always be filled with challenges. It's best to admit this to yourself and decide to be happy anyway. One of my favorite quotes comes from Alfred D' Souza. He said, "For a long time it had seemed to me that life was about to begin—real life. But there was always some obstacle in the way, something to be got through first, some unfinished business, time still to be served, a debt to be paid. Then life would begin. At last it dawned on me that these obstacles were my life." This perspective has helped me to see that there is no way *to* happiness. Happiness *is* the way.

70.

Remember that You Become
What You Practice Most

Repeated practice is one of the most basic principles of most spiritual and meditative paths. In other words, whatever you practice most is what you will become. If you are in the habit of being uptight whenever life isn't quite right, repeatedly reacting to criticism by defending yourself, insisting on being right, allowing your thinking to snowball in response to adversity, or acting like life is an emergency, then, unfortunately, your life will be a reflection of this type of practice. You will be frustrated because, in a sense, you have practiced being frustrated.

Likewise, however, you can choose to bring forth in yourself qualities of compassion, patience, kindness, humility, and peace—again, through what you practice. I guess it's safe to say that practice makes perfect. It makes sense, then, to be careful what you practice.

This isn't to suggest that you make your entire life into a great big project where the goal is to be constantly improving yourself. Only that it's immensely helpful to become conscious of your own habits, both internal and external. Where is your attention? How do you spend your time? Are you cultivating habits that are helpful to your stated goals? Is what you say you want your life to stand for consistent with what your life really stands for? Simply asking yourself these and other important questions, and answering them honestly, helps to determine which strategies will be most useful to you. Have you always said to yourself, "I'd like to spend more time by myself" or "I've always wanted to learn to meditate," yet somehow you've never found the time? Sadly, many people spend far more time washing their car or watching reruns of television shows they don't even enjoy than they do making time for aspects of life that nurture their hearts. If you remember that what you practice you will become, you may begin choosing different types of practice.

71.

Quiet the Mind

Pascal said, "All of humanity's problems stem from man's inability to sit quietly in a room alone." I'm not sure I would go quite this far, but I am certain that a quiet mind is the foundation of inner peace. And inner peace translates into outer peace.

Although there are many techniques for quieting the mind, such as reflection, deep breathing, contemplation, and visualization, the most universally accepted and regularly used technique is meditation. In as little as five to ten minutes a day, you can train your mind to be still and quiet. This stillness can be incorporated into your daily life, making you less reactive and irritable, and giving you greater perspective to see things as small stuff rather than as emergencies. Meditation teaches you to be calm by giving you the experience of absolute relaxation. It teaches you to be at peace.

There are many different forms and variations of meditation. Essentially, however, meditation involves emptying your mind. Usually, meditation is done alone in a quiet environment. You close your eyes and focus your attention on your breath—in and out, in and out. As thoughts enter your mind, you gently let them go and bring your attention back to your breath. Do this over and over again. Over time, you'll train yourself to keep your attention on your breath as you gently dismiss any stray thoughts.

You'll quickly discover that meditation isn't easy. You will notice that your mind will fill with thoughts the moment you attempt to keep it still. It's rare for a beginner to be able to focus attention for more than a few seconds. The trick to becoming an effective meditator is to be gentle on yourself and to be consistent. Don't be discouraged. A few minutes each day will reap tremendous benefits, over time. You can probably find a meditation class in your community. Or, if you prefer, you can learn from a book or, better yet, an audiotape. (It's hard to read with your eyes closed.) My favorite resource is Larry Le Shan's *How to Meditate*, available in both book and audio format. I don't know many people I would consider to be at peace with themselves who haven't spent at least a little time experimenting with meditation.

72.

Take Up Yoga

Like meditation, yoga is an extremely popular and effective method for becoming a more relaxed, easygoing person. For centuries, yoga has been used to clear and free the mind, giving people feelings of ease and equanimity. It's easy to do and takes only a few minutes a day. What's more, people of virtually any age and fitness level can participate. I once took a class at the health club that included both a ten-year-old boy and an eighty-seven-year-old man. Yoga is noncompetitive in nature. You work and progress at your own speed and comfort level.

Although yoga is physical in nature, its benefits are both physical and emotional. On the physical side, yoga strengthens the muscles and the spine, creating flexibility and ease of motion. On the emotional side, yoga is a tremendous stress reducer. It balances the body-mind-spirit connection, giving you a feeling of ease and peace.

Yoga is practiced by engaging in a series of stretches, both gentle and challenging. The stretches are designed to open the body and lengthen the spine. The stretches focus on very specific, usually tight and constricted places—the neck, back, hips, legs, and spine. While you are stretching, you are also concentrating, focusing your attention on what you are doing.

The effects of yoga are truly amazing. After only a few minutes, you feel more alive and open, peaceful and relaxed. Your mind is clear. The rest of your day is easier and more focused. I used to believe that I was too busy to practice yoga. I felt I didn't have time. I'm now certain that the opposite is true—I don't have time not to practice yoga. It's too important not to do. It keeps me feeling young and energized. It's also a wonderful and peaceful way to spend time with family and/or friends. Rather than watching television together, my two daughters and I often flip on a yoga video and spend a few minutes stretching together.

Like meditation, it's easy to find a local class at a community center, the YMCA, or health club. If you prefer to learn from a book, my favorite is *Richard Hittleman's Yoga Twenty-eight-Day Exercise Plan*. There are also many fine videos you can learn from as well as a magazine dedicated solely to yoga called *Yoga Journal*.

73.

Make Service an Integral Part
of Your Life

To become a kinder, more loving individual requires action. Yet, ironically, there is nothing specific you have to do, no prescription to follow. Rather, most genuine acts of kindness and generosity seem natural; they stem from a type of thinking where service and giving have been integrated into the person's thought process.

Several teachers and philosophers that I have learned from have suggested that I begin my day by asking myself the question, "How can I be of service?" I have found this to be useful in reminding me of the multitude of ways that I can be helpful to others. When I take the time to ask this question, I find answers popping up all day long.

If one of your goals is to be of help to others, you will find the most appropriate ways. Your chances to be of service are endless. Sometimes the best way that I can be of service is to offer my home to a friend (or even a stranger) in need. Other times, it's to give my seat to an elderly person on the train, help a youngster across the monkey bars, speak to a group, write a book, help out in my daughter's school, write a check to a charity, or pick up litter on the road. The key, I believe, is to remember that being of service isn't a one-time effort. It's not doing something nice for someone and then wondering why others aren't being nice too, or doing things for us. Instead, a life of service *is* a lifelong process, a way of thinking about life. Does the trash need to be taken out? If so, go ahead and take it out even if it's not your turn. Is someone you know being difficult? Maybe they need a hug or someone to listen to them. Are you aware of a charity that is in trouble? Could you possibly give a little extra this month?

I have learned that the best way to be of service is often very simple—it's those little, quiet, often unnoticed acts of kindness that I can choose on a daily basis—being supportive of a new endeavor by my spouse, or simply taking the time and energy to listen. I know that I have a long way to go toward my goal of becoming a more selfless person. However, I also know that as I have attempted to integrate service into my life, I have felt better and better about the way I choose to live. There is an ancient saying, "Giving is its own reward." It's really true. When you give, you also receive. In fact, what you receive is directly proportional to what you give. As you give more freely of yourself in your own unique ways, you will experience more feelings of peace than you ever thought possible. Everyone wins, especially you.

74.

Do a Favor and Don't Ask For,
or Expect, One in Return

This is a strategy that can help you practice integrating service into your life. It will show you how easy it is and how good it feels to do something nice for someone without expecting anything in return.

So often, either consciously or unconsciously, we want something from others, especially when we have done something for them—"I cleaned the bathroom, she should clean the kitchen." Or, "I took care of her child last week, she should offer this week." It's almost as though we keep score of our own good deeds rather than remembering that giving *is* its own reward.

When you do something nice for someone, just to do it, you'll notice (if you're quiet enough inside yourself) a beautiful feeling of ease and peace. Just as vigorous exercise releases endorphins in your brain that make you feel good physically, your acts of loving-kindness release the emotional equivalent. Your reward is the feeling you receive in knowing that you participated in an act of kindness. You don't need something in return or even a "thank you." In fact, you don't even need to let the person know what you have done.

What interferes with this peaceful feeling is our expectation of reciprocity. Our own thoughts interfere with our peaceful feelings as they clutter our minds, as we get caught up in what we think we want or need. The solution is to notice your "I want something in return" thoughts and gently dismiss them. In the absence of these thoughts, your positive feelings will return.

See if you can think of something really thoughtful to do for someone, and don't expect anything in return—whether it's surprising your spouse with a clean garage or organized desk, mowing your neighbor's lawn, or coming home early from work to give your spouse a break from the kids. When you complete your favor, see if you can tap into the warm feeling of knowing you have done something really nice without expecting anything from the person you have just helped. If you practice, I think you'll discover that the feelings themselves are reward enough.

75.

Think of Your Problems
as Potential Teachers

M ost people would agree that one of the greatest sources of stress in our lives is our problems. To a certain degree this is true. A more accurate assessment, however, is that the amount of stress we feel has more to do with how we relate to our problems than it does with the problems themselves. In other words, how much of a problem do we make our problems? Do we see them as emergencies, or as potential teachers?

Problems come in many shapes, sizes, and degrees of seriousness, but all have one thing in common: They present us with something that we wish were different. The more we struggle with our problems and the more we want them to go away, the worse they seem and the more stress they cause us.

Ironically, and luckily, the opposite is also true. When we accept our problems as an inevitable part of life, when we look at them as potential teachers, it's as if a weight has been lifted off our shoulders.

Think of a problem that you have struggled with for quite

some time. How have you dealt with this problem up until now? If you're like most, you've probably struggled with it, mentally rehearsed it, analyzed it again and again, but have come up short. Where has all this struggle led you? Probably to even more confusion and stress.

Now think of the same problem in a new way. Rather than push away the problem and resist it, try to embrace it. Mentally, hold the problem near to your heart. Ask yourself what valuable lesson(s) this problem might be able to teach you. Could it be teaching you to be more careful or patient? Does it have anything to do with greed, envy, carelessness, or forgiveness? Or something equally powerful? Whatever problems you are dealing with, chances are they could be thought of in a softer way that includes a genuine desire to learn from them. When you hold your problems in this light, they soften like a clenched fist that is opening. Give this strategy a try, and I think you'll agree that most problems aren't the emergencies we think they are. And usually, once we learn what we need to learn, they begin to go away.

76.

Get Comfortable Not Knowing

There once was a village that had among its people a very wise old man. The villagers trusted this man to provide them answers to their questions and concerns.

One day, a farmer from the village went to the wise man and said in a frantic tone, "Wise man, help me. A horrible thing has happened. My ox has died and I have no animal to help me plow my field! Isn't this the worst thing that could have possibly happened?" The wise old man replied, "Maybe so, maybe not." The man hurried back to the village and reported to his neighbors that the wise man had gone mad. Surely this *was* the worst thing that could have happened. Why couldn't he see this?

The very next day, however, a strong, young horse was seen near the man's farm. Because the man had no ox to rely on, he had the idea to catch the horse to replace his ox—and he did. How joyful the farmer was. Plowing the field had never been easier. He went back to the wise man to apologize. "You were right, wise man. Losing my ox wasn't the worst thing that could have happened. It was a blessing in disguise! I never would have captured my new horse had that not happened. You must agree that this is the *best* thing that could have happened." The wise man replied once again, "Maybe so, maybe not." Not again, thought the farmer. Surely the wise man had gone mad now.

But, once again, the farmer did not know what was to happen. A few days later the farmer's son was riding the horse and was thrown off. He broke his leg and would not be able to help with the crop. Oh no, thought the man. Now we will starve to death. Once again, the farmer went to the wise man. This time he said, "How did you know that capturing my horse was not a good thing? You were right again. My son is injured and won't be able to help with the crop. This time I'm sure that this is the *worst* thing that could have possibly happened. You must agree this time." But, just as he had done before, the wise man calmly looked at the farmer and in a compassionate tone replied once again, "Maybe so, maybe not." Enraged that the wise man could be so ignorant, the farmer stormed back to the village.

The next day troops arrived to take every able-bodied man to the war that had just broken out. The farmer's son was the only young man in the village who didn't have to go. He would live, while the others would surely die.

The moral of this story provides a powerful lesson. The truth is, we *don't* know what's going to happen—we just think we do. Often we make a big deal out of something. We blow up scenarios in our minds about all the terrible things that are going to happen. Most of the time we are wrong. If we keep our cool and stay open to possibilities, we can be reasonably certain that, eventually, all will be well. Remember: maybe so, maybe not.

77.

Acknowledge the Totality of Your Being

Z orba the Greek was said to have described himself as "the whole catastrophe." The truth is, we're all the whole catastrophe, only we wish that we weren't. We deny the parts of ourselves that we deem unacceptable rather than accepting the fact that we're all less than perfect.

One of the reasons it's important to accept all aspects of yourself is that it allows you to be easier on yourself, more compassionate. When you act or feel insecure, rather than pretending to be "together," you can open to the truth and say to yourself, "I'm feeling frightened and that's okay." If you're feeling a little jealous, greedy, or angry, rather than deny or bury your feelings, you can open to them, which helps you move through them quickly and grow beyond them. When you no longer think of your negative feelings as a big deal, or as something to fear, you will no longer be as frightened by them. When you open to the totality of your being you no longer have to pretend that your life is perfect, or even hope that it will be. Instead you can accept yourself as you are, right now.

When you acknowledge the less than perfect parts of yourself, something magical begins to happen. Along with the negative, you'll also begin to notice the positive, the wonderful aspects of yourself that you may not have given yourself credit for, or perhaps even been aware of. You'll notice that while you may, at times, act with self-interest in mind, at other times you're incredibly selfless. Sometimes you may act insecure or frightened, but most often you are courageous. While you can certainly get uptight, you can also be quite relaxed.

Opening to the totality of your being is like saying to yourself, "I may not be perfect, but I'm okay just the way I am." When negative characteristics arise you can begin to recognize them as part of a bigger picture. Rather than judging and evaluating yourself simply because you're human, see if you can treat yourself with loving-kindness and great acceptance. You may indeed be "the whole catastrophe," but you can relax about it. So are the rest of us.

78.

Cut Yourself Some Slack

Each of the strategies in this book is geared toward helping you become more relaxed, peaceful, and loving. One of the most important pieces of this puzzle, however, is to remember that your goal is to stay relaxed, to not get too worked up or concerned about how you are doing. Practice the strategies, keep them in mind, yet don't worry about being perfect. Cut yourself some slack! There will be many times when you lose it, when you revert to being uptight, frustrated, stressed, and reactive—get used to it. When you do, it's okay. Life is a process—just one thing after another. When you lose it, just start again.

One of the most common mistakes I see when people are attempting to become more inwardly peaceful is that they become frustrated by little setbacks. An alternative is to see your mistakes as learning opportunities, ways to navigate your growth and perspective. Say to yourself, "Woops, I lost it again. Oh well, next time I'll handle it differently." Over time, you'll notice drastic changes in your responses to life, but it won't happen all at once.

I once heard of a proposed book title that sums up the message of this strategy: *I'm Not Okay, You're Not Okay, and That's Okay.* Give yourself a break. No one is going to bat 100 percent, or even close to it. All that's important is that, generally speaking, you are doing your best and that you are moving in the right direction. When you can learn to keep your perspective and to stay loving toward yourself, even when you prove you are human, you'll be well on your way to a happier life.

79.

Stop Blaming Others

When something doesn't meet our expectations, many of us operate with the assumption, "When in doubt, it must be someone else's fault." You can see this assumption in action almost everywhere you look—something is missing, so someone else must have moved it; the car isn't working right, so the mechanic must have repaired it incorrectly; your expenses exceed your income, so your spouse must be spending too much money; the house is a mess, so you must be the only person doing your part; a project is late, so your colleagues at work must not have done their share—and on and on it goes.

This type of blaming thinking has become extremely common in our culture. On a personal level, it has led us to believe that we are never completely responsible for our own actions, problems, or happiness. On a societal level, it has led to frivolous lawsuits and ridiculous excuses that get criminals off the hook. When we are in the habit of blaming others, we will blame others for our anger, frustration, depression, stress, and unhappiness.

In terms of personal happiness, you *cannot* be peaceful while at the same time blaming others. Surely there are times when other people and/or circumstances contribute to our problems, but it is we who must rise to the occasion and take responsibility for our own happiness. Circumstances don't make a person, they reveal him or her.

As an experiment, notice what happens when you stop blaming others for anything and everything in your life. This doesn't mean you don't hold people accountable for their actions, but that you hold *yourself* accountable for your own happiness and for your reactions to other people and the circumstances around you. When the house is a mess, rather than assuming you're the only person doing your part, clean it up! When you're over budget, figure out where *you* can spend less money. Most important, when you're unhappy, remind yourself that only you can make yourself happy.

Blaming others takes an enormous amount of mental energy. It's a "drag-me-down" mind-set that creates stress and disease. Blaming makes you feel powerless over your own life because your happiness is contingent on the actions and behavior of others, which you can't control. When you stop blaming others, you will regain your sense of personal power. You will see yourself as a choice maker. You will know that when you are upset, you are playing a key role in the creation of your own feelings. This means that you can also play a key role in creating new, more positive feelings. Life is a great deal more fun and much easier to manage when you stop blaming others. Give it a try and see what happens.

80.

Become an Early Riser

I have seen this simple, practical strategy help many people discover a more peaceful, even a more meaningful life.

So many people wake up, rush to get ready, grab a cup of coffee, and charge out the door to work. After working all day, they return home, tired. The same is usually true for men and women who stay home with their children: They get up just in time to start doing things for the kids. There is virtually no time for anything else. Whether you work, raise a family, or both, for the most part you are too tired to enjoy any time left for you. As a solution to the tiredness, the assumption is often made, "I'd better get as much sleep as I can." So, your free time is spent sleeping. For many people this creates a deep longing in the heart. Surely there must be more to life than work, children, and sleep!

Another way of looking at your fatigue is to consider that a lack of fulfillment and a sense of being overwhelmed both contribute to your tiredness. And, contrary to popular logic, a little *less* sleep and a little more time for you might be just what you need to combat your sense of fatigue.

An hour or two that is reserved just for you—*before* your day begins—is an incredible way to improve your life. I usually get up between 3 and 4 in the morning. After a quiet cup of coffee, I usually spend some time doing yoga and a few minutes of meditation. After that, I will usually go upstairs and write for a while, but I also have time to read a chapter or two in whatever book I'm enjoying. Sometimes I'll just sit for a few minutes and do nothing. Virtually every day, I stop whatever I'm doing to enjoy the sunrise as it comes up over the mountain. The phone never rings, no one is asking me to do anything for them, and there is nothing I absolutely have to do. It's by far the most quiet time of the day.

By the time my wife and children wake up, I feel as though I've had a full day of enjoyment. No matter how busy I am that day or whatever demands there are on my time, I know I've had "my time." I never feel ripped off (as so many people unfortunately do), as if my life isn't my own. I believe this makes me more available for my wife and children, as well as my clients at work and other people who depend on me.

Many people have told me that this one shift in their routine was the single most important change they have ever made in their lives. For the first time ever, they are able to participate in those quiet activities they never found the time to do. All of a sudden, the books are getting read, the meditation gets done, the sunrise is appreciated. The fulfillment you experience more than makes up for any sleep you miss out on. If you must, turn off the television at night and get to sleep an hour or two earlier.

81.

When Trying to Be Helpful, Focus on Little Things

Mother Teresa once said, "We cannot do great things on this earth. We can only do little things with great love." Sometimes our grandiose plans to do great things at some later time interfere with our chances to do little things right now. A friend once told me, "I want my life to be about service, but I can't do anything yet. Someday, when I'm really successful, I'll do lots of things for others." Meanwhile, there are hungry people in the streets, elderly people who could use some company, mothers who need help with their children, people who can't read, neighbors whose homes need paint, streets with litter, people who need to be listened to, and thousands and thousands of other little things that need to be done.

Mother Teresa was right. We can't change the world, but to make the world a brighter place we don't need to. All we really have to do is focus on those little acts of kindness, things we can do right now. My favorite ways to be of service are to develop my own helping rituals and to practice random acts of kindness—almost always little things that give me enormous satisfaction and peace of mind. Often the most appreciated acts of kindness aren't the million-dollar grants from giant corporations but the one hour of volunteer work in a home for the elderly or the five-dollar gift from someone who can't afford anything at all.

If we focus on how little difference our acts of kindness really make in the scheme of things, surely we will end up frustrated—and will probably use our hopelessness as an excuse to do nothing. If, however, we take great care in doing something—anything—we will feel the joy of giving and will help to make our world just a little bit brighter.

82.

Remember, One Hundred Years from Now, All New People

My good friend Patti recently shared this bit of wisdom with me that she learned from one of her favorite authors. It has added a great deal of perspective to my life.

In the scheme of things, one hundred years isn't all that long a time. However, one thing's for sure: A hundred years from now we will all be gone from this planet. And when kept in mind, this idea can fill us with needed perspective during times of perceived crisis or stress.

If you have a flat tire or lock yourself out of your house, what's it going to mean one hundred years from now? How about if someone acted unkindly toward you or if you had to stay up most of the night working? What if your house didn't get cleaned or your computer breaks down? Suppose you can't afford to go on a much needed vacation, buy a new car, or move to a larger apartment? All of these things and most others are brought into a deeper perspective when looked at with a hundred-year view.

Just this morning I found myself at a mental fork in the road, about to get uptight about a mini crisis at work. There was a double booking and two people showed up at the same time for the same appointment. What saved me from getting overly stressed and too uptight was remembering that one hundred years from now, no one will remember this moment, no one will care. I calmly took responsibility for the error and one of the people was happy to reschedule. As usual, this was "small stuff" that could easily have been turned into "big stuff."

83.

Lighten Up

These days, it seems that almost all of us are too serious. My older daughter often says to me, "Daddy, you've got that serious look again." Even those of us who are committed to nonseriousness are probably too serious. People are frustrated and uptight about virtually everything—being five minutes late, having someone else show up five minutes late, being stuck in traffic, witnessing someone look at us wrong or say the wrong thing, paying bills, waiting in line, overcooking a meal, making an honest mistake—you name it, we all lose perspective over it.

The root of being uptight is our unwillingness to accept life as being different, in any way, from our expectations. Very simply, we want things to be a certain way but they're *not* a certain way. Life is simply as it is. Perhaps Benjamin Franklin said it best: "Our limited perspective, our hopes and fears become our measure of life, and when circumstances don't fit our ideas, they become our difficulties." We spend our lives wanting things, people, and events to be just as we want them to be—and when they're not, we fight and we suffer.

The first step in recovering from overseriousness is to admit that you have a problem. You have to want to change, to become more easygoing. You have to see that your own uptightness is largely of your own creation—it's composed of the way you have set up your life and the way you react to it.

The next step is to understand the link between your expectations and your frustration level. Whenever you expect something to be a certain way and it isn't, you're upset and you suffer. On the other hand, when you let go of your expectations, when you accept life as it is, you're free. To hold on is to be serious and uptight. To let go is to lighten up.

A good exercise is to try to approach a single day without expectations. Don't expect people to be friendly. When they're not, you won't be surprised or bothered. If they are, you'll be delighted. Don't expect your day to be problem free. Instead, as problems come up, say to yourself, "Ah, another hurdle to overcome." As you approach your day in this manner you'll notice how graceful life can be. Rather than fighting against life, you'll be dancing with it. Pretty soon, with practice, you'll lighten up your entire life. And when you lighten up, life is a lot more fun.

84.

Nurture a Plant

At first glance this may seem like a strange or superficial suggestion. What good could it possibly do to nurture a plant?

One of the goals of spiritual life and one of the requirements of inner peace is to learn to love unconditionally. The problem is, it's really hard to love a person, any person, unconditionally. The person we are trying to love inevitably says or does the wrong thing, or fails to meet our expectations in some way. So, we get upset and put conditions on our love: "I'll love you, but you have to change. You must act the way I want you to act."

Some people are better at loving their pets than the people in their lives. But to love a pet unconditionally is hard too. What happens when your dog wakes you up with unnecessary barking in the middle of the night or ruins your favorite carpet with an accident? Do you love him just as much? My children have a bunny. It was really hard to love that bunny when he chewed a hole in my beautifully crafted wooden gate!

A plant, however, is easy to love just the way it is. Therefore, nurturing a plant offers us an excellent opportunity to practice unconditional love.

Why does virtually every spiritual tradition advocate unconditional love? Because love has such transformational power. Unconditional love brings forth peaceful feelings in both the giver and the receiver.

Select a plant, indoor or outdoor, that you will see every day. Practice taking care of and loving that plant as if it were your baby (it's easier to care for your plant than your baby—no sleepless nights, no diapers, no crying). Talk to your plant, tell it how much you love it. Love your plant whether it blooms or not, whether it lives or dies. Just love it. Notice how you feel as you offer this plant your unconditional love. When you offer this type of love you're never agitated, irritated, or hurried. You're simply in a loving space. Practice this type of love each time you see your plant, at least once a day.

After a short while, you'll be able to extend your loving-kindness beyond your plant as well. As you notice how good it feels to love, see if you can offer a similar love to the people in your life. Practice not needing them to change or be different to receive your love. Love them just the way they are. Your plant can be a wonderful teacher—showing you the power of love.

85.

Transform Your Relationship
to Your Problems

Obstacles and problems are a part of life. True happiness comes not when we get rid of all of our problems, but when we change our relationship to them, when we see our problems as a potential source of awakening, opportunities to practice patience, and to learn. Perhaps the most basic principle of spiritual life is that our problems are the best places to practice keeping our hearts open.

Certainly some problems need to be solved. Many others, however, are problems we create for ourselves by struggling to make our life different than it actually is. Inner peace is accomplished by understanding and accepting the inevitable contradictions of life—the pain and pleasure, success and failure, joy and sorrow, births and deaths. Problems can teach us to be gracious, humble, and patient.

In the Buddhist tradition, difficulties are considered to be so important to a life of growth and peace that a Tibetan prayer actually asks for them. It says, "Grant that I may be given appropriate difficulties and sufferings on this journey so that my heart may be truly awakened and my practice of liberation and universal compassion may be truly fulfilled." It is felt that when life is too easy, there are fewer opportunities for genuine growth.

I wouldn't go so far as to recommend that you seek out problems. I would, however, suggest that if you spend less time running away from problems and trying to rid yourself of them—and more time accepting problems as an inevitable, natural, even important part of life—you will soon discover that life can be more of a dance and less of a battle. This philosophy of acceptance is the root of going with the flow.

86.

The Next Time You Find Yourself in an Argument, Rather than Defend Your Position, See if You Can See the Other Point of View First

It's interesting to consider that when you disagree with someone, the person you are disagreeing with is every bit as certain of his or her position as you are of yours. Yet we always take sides—ours! This is our ego's way of refusing to learn anything new. It's also a habit that creates a lot of unnecessary stress.

The first time I consciously tried the strategy of seeing the other point of view first, I found out something truly wonderful: It didn't hurt, and it brought me closer to the person with whom I was disagreeing.

Suppose a friend says to you, "Liberals [or conservatives] are the major cause of our social problems." Rather than automatically defending your own position (whatever it is), see if you can learn something new. Say to your friend, "Tell me why you think that's true." Don't say this with a hidden agenda or in preparation to defend or prove your position, but simply to learn a different point of view. Don't try to correct or make your friend see how he is wrong. Let your friend have the satisfaction of being right. Practice being a good listener.

Contrary to popular belief, this attitude does not make you weak. It doesn't mean you aren't passionate about your beliefs, or that you're admitting that you're wrong. You're simply trying to see another point of view—you're seeking first to understand. It takes enormous energy to constantly prove a rigid position. On the other hand, it takes no energy to allow someone else to be right. In fact, it's outright energizing.

When you understand other positions and points of view, several wonderful things begin to happen. First, you often learn something new. You expand your horizons. Second, when the person you are talking to feels listened to, he or she will appreciate and respect you far more than when you habitually jump in with your own position. Jumping in only makes him or her more determined and defensive. Almost always, if *you* are softer, the other person will be softer too. It might not happen right away, but in time, it will. By seeking first to understand, you are putting your love and respect for the person to whom you are speaking above your need to be right. You are practicing a form of unconditional love. A side benefit is that the person you are speaking to may even listen to your point of view. While there is no guarantee that he will listen to you, one thing is guaranteed: If you don't listen, he or she won't. By being the first person to reach out and listen, you stop the spiral of stubbornness.

87.

Redefine a "Meaningful Accomplishment"

Sometimes it's easy to get carried away with our so-called accomplishments. We spend our lifetimes collecting achievements, earning praise and recognition, and seeking approval—so much so that we lose sight of what is truly meaningful.

If you ask the average person (as I have done many times), "What is a meaningful accomplishment?" the typical responses will be things like, "Achieving a long-term goal," "earning lots of money," "winning a game," "getting a promotion," "being the best," "earning praise," and so forth. The emphasis is almost always on the *external* aspects of life—things that happen outside of ourselves. Certainly, there is nothing wrong with these types of accomplishments—they are way of keeping score and improving our circumstances. They are not, however, the most important types of accomplishments if your primary goal is one of happiness and inner peace. Seeing your photograph in the local newspaper may be a nice thing to achieve but isn't as meaningful as learning to stay centered in the face of adversity. Yet many people would point to their photo in the paper as being a great accomplishment, but wouldn't necessarily think of "staying centered" as an accomplishment at all. Where are our priorities?

If being peaceful and loving are among your primary goals, then why not redefine your most meaningful accomplishments as being those that support and measure qualities such as kindness and happiness?

I think of my most meaningful accomplishments as stemming from inside myself: Was I kind to myself and others? Did I overreact to a challenge, or was I calm and collected? Am I happy? Did I hold on to anger or was I able to let go and move on? Was I too stubborn? Did I forgive? These questions, and others like them, remind us that the true measure of our success comes not from what we do, but from who we are and how much love we have in our hearts.

Rather than being consumed exclusively with external accomplishments, try putting more emphasis on what's really important. When you redefine what it means to achieve a meaningful accomplishment, it helps you to stay on your path.

88.

Listen to Your Feelings
(They Are Trying to Tell You Something)

Y ou have at your disposal a foolproof guidance system to navigate you through life. This system, which consists solely of your own feelings, lets you know whether you are off track and headed toward unhappiness and conflict—or on track, headed toward peace of mind. Your feelings act as a barometer, letting you know what your internal weather is like.

When you're not caught up in your thinking, taking things too seriously, your feelings will be generally positive. They will be affirming that you are using your thinking to your advantage. No mental adjustment needs to be made.

When your experience of life is other than pleasant—when you're feeling angry, resentful, depressed, stressed out, frustrated, and so forth, your warning system of feelings kicks in like a red flag to remind you that you are off track, that it's time to ease up on your thinking, you've lost perspective. Mental adjustment does need to be made. You can think of your negative feelings in the same way you think of the warning lights on the dashboard of your car. When flashing, they let you know that it's time to ease up.

Contrary to popular belief, negative feelings don't need to be studied and analyzed. When you analyze your negative feelings, you'll usually end up with more of them to contend with.

The next time you're feeling bad, rather than getting stuck in "analysis paralysis," wondering why you feel the way you do, see if instead you can use your feelings to guide you back in the direction toward serenity. Don't pretend that the negative feelings don't exist, but try to recognize that the reason you're feeling sad, angry, stressed, or whatever is that you are taking life too seriously—you are "sweating the small stuff." Instead of rolling up your sleeves and fighting life, back off, take a few deep breaths, and relax. Remember, life isn't an emergency unless you make it so.

89.

If Someone Throws You the Ball,
You Don't Have to Catch It

My best friend, Benjamin Shield, taught me this valuable lesson. Often our inner struggles come from our tendency to jump on board someone else's problem; someone throws you a concern and you assume you must catch it, and respond. For example, suppose you're really busy when a friend calls in a frantic tone and says, "My mother is driving me crazy. What should I do?" Rather than saying, "I'm really sorry but I don't know what to suggest," you automatically catch the ball and try to solve the problem. Then later, you feel stressed or resentful that you are behind schedule and that everyone seems to be making demands on you. It's easy to lose sight of your willing participation in the dramas of your own life.

Remembering that you don't have to catch the ball is a very effective way to reduce the stress in your life. When your friend calls, you *can* drop the ball, meaning you don't have to participate simply because he or she is attempting to lure you in. If you don't take the bait, the person will probably call someone else to see if they will become involved.

This doesn't mean you never catch the ball, only that it's your choice to do so. Neither does this mean that you don't care about your friend, or that you're crass or unhelpful. Developing a more tranquil outlook on life requires that we know our own limits and that we take responsibility for our part in the process. Most of us get balls thrown at us many times each day—at work, from our children, friends, neighbors, salespeople, even strangers. If I caught all the balls thrown in my direction, I would certainly go crazy—and I suspect that you would too! The key is to know when we're catching another ball so that we won't feel victimized, resentful, or overwhelmed.

Even something terribly simple like answering your phone when you're really too busy to talk is a form of catching the ball. By answering the phone, you are willingly taking part in an interaction that you may not have the time, energy, or mind-set for at the present time. By simply not answering the phone, you are taking responsibility for your own peace of mind. The same idea applies to being insulted or criticized. When someone throws an idea or comment in your direction, you can catch it and feel hurt, or you can drop it and go on with your day.

The idea of "not catching the ball" simply because it's thrown to you is a powerful tool to explore. I hope you'll experiment with this one. You may find that you catch the ball a lot more than you think you do.

90.

One More Passing Show

This is a strategy that I have recently adopted into my own life. It's a subtle reminder that everything—the good and bad, pleasure and pain, approval and disapproval, achievements and mistakes, fame and shame—all come and go. Everything has a beginning and an ending and that's the way it's supposed to be.

Every experience you have ever had is over. Every thought you've ever had, started and finished. Every emotion and mood you've experienced has been replaced by another. You've been happy, sad, jealous, depressed, angry, in love, shamed, proud, and every other conceivable human feeling. Where did they all go? The answer is, no one really knows. All we know is that, eventually, everything disappears into nothingness. Welcoming this truth into your life is the beginning of a liberating adventure.

Our disappointment comes about in essentially two ways. When we're experiencing pleasure we want it to last forever. It never does. Or, when we're experiencing pain, we want it to go away—now. It usually doesn't. Unhappiness is the result of struggling against the natural flow of experience.

It's enormously helpful to experiment with the awareness that life is just one thing after another. One present moment followed by another present moment. When something is happening that we enjoy, know that while it's wonderful to experience the happiness it brings, it will eventually be replaced by something else, a different type of moment. If that's okay with you, you'll feel peace even when the moment changes. And if you're experiencing some type of pain or displeasure, know that this too shall pass. Keeping this awareness close to your heart is a wonderful way to maintain your perspective, even in the face of adversity. It's not always easy, but it is usually helpful.

91.

Fill Your Life with Love

I don't know anyone who doesn't want a life filled with love. In order for this to happen, the effort must start within us. Rather than waiting for other people to provide the love we desire, *we* must be a vision and a source of love. We must tap into our own loving-kindness in order to set an example for others to follow suit.

It has been said that "the shortest distance between two points is an intention." This is certainly true with regard to a life filled with love. The starting point or foundation of a life filled with love is the desire and commitment to be a source of love. Our attitude, choices, acts of kindness, and willingness to be the first to reach out will take us toward this goal.

The next time you find yourself frustrated at the lack of love in your own life or at the lack of love in the world, try an experiment. Forget about the world and other people for a few minutes. Instead, look into your own heart. Can you become a source of greater love? Can you think loving thoughts for yourself and others? Can you extend these loving thoughts outward toward the rest of the world—even to people whom you feel don't deserve it?

By opening your heart to the possibility of greater love, and by making yourself a source of love (rather than getting love) as a top priority, you will be taking an important step in getting the love you desire. You'll also discover something truly re-markable. The more love you give, the more you will receive. As you put more emphasis on being a loving person, which is something you can control—and less emphasis on receiving love, which is something you can't control—you'll find that you have plenty of love in your life. Soon you'll discover one of the greatest secrets in the world: Love is its own reward.

92.

Realize the Power of Your Own Thoughts

If you were to become aware of only one mental dynamic, the most important one to know about would be the relationship between your thinking and the way you feel.

It's important to realize that you are constantly thinking. Don't be fooled into believing that you are already aware of this fact! Think, for a moment, about your breathing. Until this moment, when you are reading this sentence, you had certainly lost sight of the fact that you were doing it. The truth is, unless you are out of breath, you simply forget that it's occurring.

Thinking works in the same way. Because you're always doing it, it's easy to forget that it's happening, and it becomes invisible to you. Unlike breathing, however, forgetting that you are thinking can cause some serious problems in your life, such as unhappiness, anger, inner conflicts, and stress. The reason this is true is that your thinking will always come back to you as a feeling; there is a point-to-point relationship.

Try getting angry without first having angry thoughts! Okay, now try feeling stressed out without first having stressful thoughts—or sad without sad thoughts—or jealous without thoughts of jealousy. You can't do it—it's impossible. The truth is, in order to experience a feeling, you must first have a thought that produces that feeling.

Unhappiness doesn't and can't exist on its own. Unhappiness is the feeling that accompanies negative thinking about your life. In the absence of that thinking, the unhappiness, or stress, or jealousy, can't exist. There is nothing to hold your negative feelings in place other than your own thinking. The next time you're feeling upset, notice your thinking—it will be negative. Remind yourself that it's your thinking that is negative, not your life. This simple awareness will be the first step in putting you back on the path toward happiness. It takes practice, but you can get to the point where you treat your negative thoughts in much the same way you would treat flies at a picnic: You shoo them away and get on with your day.

93.

Give Up on the Idea that "More Is Better"

We live in the most affluent culture the world has ever seen. Estimates are that although we have only 6 percent of the world's population in America, we use almost half of the natural resources. It seems to me that if more were actually better, we would live in the happiest, most satisfied culture of all time. But we don't. Not even close. In fact, we live in one of the most dissatisfied cultures on record.

It's not that having a lot of things is bad, wrong, or harmful in and of itself, only that the desire to have more and more and more is insatiable. As long as you think more is better, you'll never be satisfied.

As soon as we get something, or achieve something, most of us simply go on to the next thing—immediately. This squelches our appreciation for life and for our many blessings. I know a man, for example, who bought a beautiful home in a nice area. He was happy until the day after he moved in. Then the thrill was gone. Immediately, he wished he'd bought a bigger, nicer home. His "more is better" thinking wouldn't allow him to enjoy his new home, even for a day. Sadly, he is not unique. To varying degrees, we're all like that. It's gotten to the point that when the Dalai Lama won the Nobel Prize for Peace in 1989, one of the first questions he received from a reporter was "What's next?" It seems that whatever we do—buy a home or a car, eat a meal, find a partner, purchase some clothes, even win a prestigious honor—it's never enough.

The trick in overcoming this insidious tendency is to convince yourself that more isn't better and that the problem doesn't lie in what you don't have, but in the longing for more. Learning to be satisfied doesn't mean you can't, don't, or shouldn't ever want more than you have, only that your happiness isn't contingent on it. You can learn to be happy with what you have by becoming more present-moment oriented, by not focusing so much on what you want. As thoughts of what would make your life better enter your mind, gently remind yourself that, even if you got what you think you want, you wouldn't be one bit more satisfied, because the same mind-set that wants more now would want more then.

Develop a new appreciation for the blessings you already enjoy. See your life freshly, as if for the first time. As you develop this new awareness, you'll find that as new possessions or accomplishments enter your life, your level of appreciation will be heightened.

An excellent measure of happiness is the differential between what you have and what you want. You can spend your lifetime wanting more, always chasing happiness—or you can simply decide to consciously want less. This latter strategy is infinitely easier and more fulfilling.

94.

Keep Asking Yourself,
"What's Really Important?"

It's easy to get lost and overwhelmed in the chaos, responsibilities, and goals of life. Once overwhelmed, it's tempting to forget about and postpone that which is most near and dear to your heart. I've found that it's helpful to keep asking myself, "What's really important?"

As part of my early morning routine, I take a few seconds to ask myself this question. Reminding myself of what's really important helps me keep my priorities straight. It reminds me that, despite my multitude of responsibilities, I have a choice of what is most important in my life and where I put my greatest amount of energy—being available for my wife and children, writing, practicing my inner work, and so forth.

Despite the appearance of being overly simplistic, I have found this strategy to be immensely helpful in keeping me on track. When I take a few moments to remind myself of what's really important, I find that I'm more present-moment oriented, in less of a hurry, and that being right loses its appeal. Conversely, when I forget to remind myself of what's really important, I find that I can quickly lose sight of my priorities and, once again, get lost in my own busyness. I'll rush out the door, work late, lose my patience, skip my exercise, and do other things that are in conflict with the goals of my life.

If you regularly take a minute to check in with yourself, to ask yourself, "What's really important?" you may find that some of the choices you are making are in conflict with your own stated goals. This strategy can help you align your actions with your goals and encourage you to make more conscious, loving decisions.

95.

Trust Your Intuitive Heart

How often have you said to yourself, after the fact, "I knew I should have done that"? How often do you intuitively know something but allow yourself to think yourself out of it?

Trusting your intuitive heart means listening to and trusting that quiet inner voice that knows what it is you need to do, what actions need to be taken, or changes need to be made in your life. Many of us *don't* listen to our intuitive heart for fear that we couldn't possibly know something without thinking it through, or for fear that legitimate answers could possibly be so obvious. We say things to ourselves like, "That couldn't possibly be right" or "I couldn't possibly do that." And, as soon as we allow our thinking mind to enter into the picture, we think ourselves out of it. We then argue for our limitations, and they become ours.

If you can overcome your fear that your intuitive heart will give you incorrect answers, if you can learn to trust it, your life will become the magical adventure it was meant to be. Trusting your intuitive heart is like removing the barriers to enjoyment and wisdom. It's the way to open your eyes and your heart to your greatest source of wisdom and grace.

If you're unfamiliar with trusting your intuition, start by setting aside a little quiet time to clear your mind and listen. Ignore and dismiss any habitual, self-defeating thoughts that enter your mind and pay attention only to the calm thoughts that begin to surface. If you find that unusual yet loving thoughts are appearing in your mind, take note of them and take action. If, for example, you get the message to write or call someone you love, go ahead and do it. If your intuitive heart says you need to slow down or take more time for yourself, try to make it happen. If you're reminded of a habit that needs attention, pay attention. You'll find that when your intuition gives you messages and you respond with action, you'll often be rewarded with positive, loving experiences. Start trusting your intuitive heart today and you'll see a world of difference in your life.

96.

Be Open to "What Is"

One of the most basic spiritual principles in many philosophies is the idea of opening your heart to "what is" instead of insisting that life be a certain way. This idea is so important because much of our internal struggle stems from our desire to control life, to insist that it be different than it actually is. But life isn't always (or even rarely is) the way we would like it to be—it is simply the way it is. The greater our surrender to the truth of the moment, the greater will be our peace of mind.

When we have preconceived ideas about the way life should be, they interfere with our opportunity to enjoy or learn from the present moment. This prevents us from honoring what we are going through, which may be an opportunity for great awakening.

Rather than reacting to a child's complaining or your spouse's disapproval, try opening your heart and accepting the moment for what it is. Make it okay that they aren't acting exactly the way you would like them to. Or, if a project you have been working on is rejected, instead of feeling defeated, see if you can say to yourself, "Ah, rejection. Next time I'll get it approved." Take a deep breath and soften your response.

You open your heart in these ways, not to pretend that you enjoy complaints, disapproval, or failure, but to transcend them—to make it all right with you that life isn't performing the way you planned. If you can learn to open your heart in the midst of the difficulties of daily life, you will soon find that many of the things that have always bothered you will cease to be concerns. Your perspective will deepen. When you fight that which you struggle with, life can be quite a battle, almost like a Ping-Pong game where you are the ball. But when you surrender to the moment, accept what is going on, make it okay, more peaceful feelings will begin to emerge. Try this technique on some of the little challenges you face. Gradually you'll be able to extend the same awareness to bigger things. This is a truly powerful way to live.

97.

Mind Your Own Business

It's tough enough trying to create a life of serenity when dealing with your own mental tendencies, issues, real-life problems, habits, and the contradictions and complexities of life. But when you feel compelled to deal with other people's issues, your goal of becoming more peaceful becomes all but impossible.

How often do you find yourself saying things like, "I wouldn't do that if I were her," or "I can't believe he did that," or "What is she thinking about?" How often are you frustrated, bothered, annoyed, or concerned about things that you not only *cannot* control or be of actual help with, but are also none of your business?

This is not a prescription to avoid being of help to people. Rather, it's about knowing when to help and when to leave something alone. I used to be the type of person who would jump in and try to solve a problem without being asked. Not only did my efforts prove fruitless, they were also almost always unappreciated, and sometimes even resented. Since recovering from my need to be overly involved, my life has become much simpler. And, now that I'm not butting in where I'm not wanted, I'm far more available to be of help when I am asked or truly needed.

Minding your own business goes far beyond simply avoiding the temptation to try to solve other people's problems. It also includes eavesdropping, gossiping, talking behind other people's backs, and analyzing or trying to figure out other people. One of the major reasons most of us focus on the shortcomings or problems of others is to avoid looking at ourselves.

When you catch yourself involved where you really don't belong, congratulate yourself for having the humility and wisdom to back off. In no time at all, you'll free up tons of extra energy to focus your attention where it's truly relevant or needed.

98.

Look for the Extraordinary in the Ordinary

I heard a story about two workers who were approached by a reporter. The reporter asked the first worker, "What are you doing?" His response was to complain that he was virtually a slave, an underpaid bricklayer who spent his days wasting his time, placing bricks on top of one another.

The reporter asked the second worker the same question. His response, however, was quite different. "I'm the luckiest person in the world," he said. "I get to be a part of important and beautiful pieces of architecture. I help turn simple pieces of brick into exquisite masterpieces."

They were both right.

The truth is, we see in life what we want to see. If you search for ugliness you'll find plenty of it. If you want to find fault with other people, your career, or the world in general, you'll certainly be able to do so. But the opposite is also true. If you look for the extraordinary in the ordinary, you can train yourself to see it. This bricklayer sees cathedrals within pieces of brick. The question is, can you? Can you see the extraordinary synchronicity that exists in our world; the perfection of the universe in action; the extraordinary beauty of nature; the incredible miracle of human life? To me, it's all a matter of intention. There is so much to be grateful for, so much to be in awe about. Life is precious and extraordinary. Put your attention on this fact and little, ordinary things will take on a whole new meaning.

99.

Schedule Time for Your Inner Work

In the field of financial planning there is a universally accepted principle that it's critical to pay yourself first, before you pay your other bills—to think of yourself as a creditor. The rationale for this financial wisdom is that if you wait to put money into savings until after everybody else is paid, there will be nothing left for you! The result is that you'll keep postponing your savings plan until it's too late to do anything about it. But, lo and behold, if you pay yourself first, somehow there will be just enough to pay everyone else too.

The identical principle is critical to implement into your program of spiritual practice. If you wait until all your chores, responsibilities, and everything else is done before you get started, it will never happen. Guaranteed.

I have found that scheduling a little time each day as if it were an actual appointment is the only way to ensure that you will take some time for yourself. You might become an early riser, for example, and schedule one hour that is reserved for reading, praying, reflecting, meditating, yoga, exercise, or however you want to use the time. How you choose to use the time is up to you. The important thing is that you do schedule the time and that you stick to it.

I had a client who actually hired a baby-sitter on a regular basis to ensure that she had the chance to do the things she felt she needed to do. Today, more than a year later, her efforts have paid enormous dividends. She's happier than she ever thought possible. She told me that there was a time that she never would have imagined hiring a baby-sitter to ensure this type of quality time for herself. Now that she has done it, she can't imagine not doing it! If you set your mind to it, you can find the time you need.

100.

Live This Day as if It Were Your Last.
It Might Be!

When are you going to die? In fifty years, twenty, ten, five, today? Last time I checked, no one had told me. I often wonder, when listening to the news, did the person who died in the auto accident on his way home from work remember to tell his family how much he loved them? Did he live well? Did he love well? Perhaps the only thing that is certain is that he still had things in his "in basket" that weren't yet done.

The truth is, none of us has any idea how long we have to live. Sadly, however, we act as if we're going to live forever. We postpone the things that, deep down, we know we want to do—telling the people we love how much we care, spending time alone, visiting a good friend, taking that beautiful hike, running a marathon, writing a heartfelt letter, going fishing with your daughter, learning to meditate, becoming a better listener, and on and on. We come up with elaborate and sophisticated rationales to justify our actions, and end up spending most of our time and energy doing things that aren't all that important. We argue for our limitations, and they become our limitations.

I felt it appropriate to end this book by suggesting that you live each day as if it were your last on this earth. I suggest this not as a prescription to be reckless or to abandon your responsibilities, but to remind you of how precious life really is. A friend of mine once said, "Life is too important to take too seriously." Ten years later, I know he was right. I hope that this book has been, and will continue to be, helpful to you. Please don't forget the most basic strategy of all, *Don't sweat the small stuff!* I will end this book by sincerely saying that I wish you well.

Treasure Yourself

Suggested Reading

The following are a few of my favorite related books that can bring additional light on the strategies listed in this book.

Bailey, Joseph. *The Serenity Principle*. San Francisco: Harper & Row, 1990

Boorstein, Sylvia. *It's Easier Than You Think*. San Francisco: HarperCollins, 1996

Carlson, Richard. *You Can Be Happy No Matter What*. San Rafael, Calif.: New World Library, 1992

——. *You Can Feel Good Again*. New York: Plume, 1993

——. *Short Cut Through Therapy*. New York: Plume, 1995

——. *Handbook for the Soul*. New York: Little, Brown, 1995

——. *Handbook for the Heart*. New York: Little, Brown, 1996

Chopra, Deepak. *The Seven Spiritual Laws of Success*. San Rafael, Calif.: New World Library, 1994

——. *Ageless Body, Timeless Mind*. New York: Harmony, 1993

Dyer, Wayne. *Real Magic*. New York: HarperCollins, 1992

——. *The Sky's the Limit*. New York: Pocket Books, 1980

——. *Your Sacred Self*. New York: Harper Paperback, 1995

——. *Your Erroneous Zones*. New York: Harper, 1976

Hay, Louise. *Life*. Carson, Calif.: Hay House, 1995

Hittleman, Richard. *Richard Hittleman's Twenty-eight-Day Yoga Exercise Plan*. New York: Bantam, 1983

Kabat-Zinn, Jon. *Wherever You Go, There You Are*. New York: Hyperion, 1994

Kornfield, Jack. *A Path with Heart*. New York: Bantam, 1993

Le Shan, Larry. *How to Meditate*. (Audio Tape) Los Angeles: Audio Renaissance, 1987

Levine, Stephen, and Ondrea Levine. *Embracing the Beloved*. New York: Anchor Books, 1995

Salzberg, Sharon. *Loving Kindness*. Boston: Shambhala, 1995

Schwartz, Tony. *What Really Matters?* New York: Bantam, 1995

Siegel, Bernie. *Love, Medicine and Miracles*. New York: Harper Perennial, 1986

Williamson, Marianne. *A Return to Love*. New York: HarperCollins, 1993